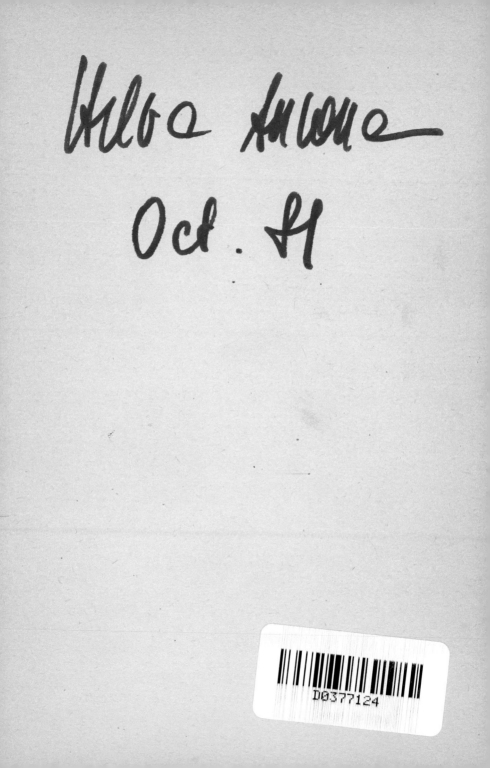

Hilda Antone

Oct. 51

GOOD WORK

BY E. F. SCHUMACHER
Good Work
A Guide for the Perplexed
Small Is Beautiful

GOOD WORK

E. F. Schumacher

Preface by George McRobie
Epilogue by Peter N. Gillingham

HARPER COLOPHON BOOKS
Harper & Row, Publishers
New York, Cambridge, Hagerstown, Philadelphia, San Francisco
London, Mexico City, São Paulo, Sydney

Portions of this work originally appeared in *The Atlantic Monthly*.

A hardcover edition of this book is published by Harper & Row, Publishers.

GOOD WORK. Copyright © 1979 by Verena Schumacher. All rights reserved. Printed in the United States of America. No part of this book may be used or reproduced in any manner whatsoever without written permission except in the case of brief quotations embodied in critical articles and reviews. For information address Harper & Row, Publishers, Inc., 10 East 53rd Street, New York, N.Y. 10022. Published simultaneously in Canada by Fitzhenry & Whiteside Limited, Toronto.

First HARPER COLOPHON edition published 1980.

ISBN: 0-06-090561-1

80 81 82 83 84 10 9 8 7 6 5 4 3 2

CONTENTS

PREFACE

When E. F. Schumacher died in September 1977, his friend Barbara Ward described him as belonging to that intensely creative minority who have changed the direction of human thought. And his two books *Small Is Beautiful* and *A Guide for the Perplexed* would alone ensure that his ideas will remain very much alive.

Fritz Schumacher's ideas were the product of a highly original and creative mind; they are generally radical, demanding drastic alterations in conventional ways of thinking and doing; and they have a universal quality about them, which appeals to countless people of different ages, classes, races, and shades of political and religious belief. But I think that there is an even more uncommon quality about his ideas, which is that they lend themselves to, indeed invite, action.

The most obvious example is his concept of intermediate technology. The critical role of technology in economic development was first brought into perspective by Schumacher in a report prepared in 1962 for the government of India. Three years later, a few of us helped him to start the Intermediate Technology Development Group in London to implement the idea, to develop and make known technologies appropriate to the needs and resources of poor people in poor communities: tools and equipment deliberately designed to be relatively small, simple, capital-saving, and environmentally nonviolent. Today, there are more than twenty similar groups operating in as many countries, and the concept has been taken up by UN agencies, governments, and voluntary organizations throughout the world. It is now recognzed as being every bit as relevant to the rich countries as to the poor.

Looking back on more than twenty years of work and friendship with Fritz Schumacher, I am struck by the consistency with which his work has changed the course of events. When he was in his thirties, while working as a farm laborer in England, he drew up a plan for a new international monetary payments clearing system, which was immediately adopted by Lord Keynes as the official U.K. government proposal on the subject. A few years later he was the principal author of the famous Beveridge report on full employment. In the 1950s and 60s as economic advisor to the British coal industry he became a persistent—and in official eyes often highly unpopular—one-man early warning system on the dangers of overdependence on oil, and the even greater dangers of nuclear power. During this time he became president of the Soil Association, a director of the Scott Bader Commonwealth, the pioneer common-ownership company in Britain, and chairman of the Intermediate Technology Group.

Once the Group was started, Schumacher continued his analysis of the impact of conventional technology and its supporting structures upon people, upon living nature, and upon nonrenewable resources. In *Small Is Beautiful* he launched a powerful attack on conventional economics and technology, and the value system supporting both. But he did not stop there; he also mapped out a sane route toward a sustainable way of life. This was followed up by *Guide for the Perplexed*, which offers the individual a philosophical framework, a guide to the moral values that underpin *Small Is Beautiful*.

The present book, *Good Work*, is compiled mainly from a series of lectures he gave in the United States during the mid-1970s, a tour during which some sixty thousand people heard him speak, and which culminated in a meeting at the White House with President Carter. Three chapters are based on earlier written essays; they have been included for their relevance to the subject of good work.

In many respects the very starting point of *Good Work* is a reflection, or rather an extension, of both earlier books. At the heart of our system of work lies our system of values, and more precisely, our view of the individual and his relationships with others. By way of illustration, consider one of the current pseudo-intellectual clichés, that work is part of the Protestant ethic and that a more enlightened view of it is (presumably) that the less work you can get away with, the better. This is a cynical and degraded view of human nature (certainly not subscribed to by any religion that I know of) because it assumes that money is the sole reason for working. Set this view against Schumacher's opening remarks in this book, in which he identifies three purposes of human work: to produce necessary and useful goods and services; to enable us to use and perfect our gifts and skills; and to serve, and collaborate with, other people, so as to "liberate ourselves from our inborn egocentricity."

You do not have to prefer this interpretation of work, and of what people and life are about, to enjoy this book; but you will enjoy the book all the more if you do, because *Good Work* is an exploration of the political, managerial, social, and economic consequences of conventional technology (and therefore of conventional values), and of alternatives that are already becoming visible: alternatives that in one way òr another support the three purposes of human work identified by Schumacher. Throughout the book he draws freely on his personal experience of involvement in such alternatives, whether of management, ownership, or technology: his work in the National Coal Board, with the Intermediate Technology Development Group, with Scott Bader, with the Soil Association, and in India, Zambia, and other developing countries.

Taken as a whole *Good Work* rounds off and makes explicit Schumacher's case that the choice of technology is one of the most critical choices now confronting any country, rich or poor. The poor countries must secure technologies appropriate to their needs and resources—intermediate technologies—if the rural masses are to be given a chance to work themselves out of poverty; but the rich countries probably stand even more in need of a new technology, smaller, capital-saving, less rapacious in its demands on raw materials, and environmentally nonviolent. The people of poor countries must be helped to raise themselves to a decent standard of living. We ourselves must also work for a more modest, nonviolent, sustainable life-style. That is surely the way toward greater equality between and within nations.

The sixty thousand people who heard Schumacher give these talks will, I am sure, be glad that the editing has been kept to a minimum; the temptation to reduce the lectures to formal essays has been resisted. The fortunate result is that here we have Fritz Schumacher at his best, on his feet, often thinking aloud, bringing his personality and creative energy, as well as his remarkable mind, to bear on what is certainly one of the most critical tasks that now confronts rich and poor societies alike: how to enable us to do creative and satisfying work, earn a decent living, live in a becoming way; and having done so, as George Kennan once put it, to leave the planet earth in a condition at least no less capable of supporting life than that in which we found it.

GEORGE McROBIE

GOOD
WORK

PROLOGUE

A recent article in the London *Times* began with these words: "Dante, when composing his visions of hell, might well have included the mindless, repetitive boredom of working on a factory assembly line. It destroys initiative and rots brains, yet millions of British workers are committed to it for most of their lives." The remarkable thing is that this statement, like countless similar ones made before it, aroused no interest: there were no hot denials or anguished agreements; no reactions at all. The strong and terrible words—"visions of hell," "destroys initiative and rots brains," and so on—attracted no reprimand that they were misstatements or overstatements, that they were irresponsible or hysterical exaggerations or subversive propaganda; no, people read them, sighed and nodded, I suppose, and moved on. Not even the ecologists, conservationists, and doomwatchers are interested in this matter. If someone had asserted that certain man-made arrangements destroyed the initiative and rotted the brains of millions of birds or seals or wild animals in the game reserves of Africa, such an assertion would have been either refuted or accepted as a serious challenge. If someone had asserted that not the minds and brains of millions of workers were being rotted but their bodies, again there would have been considerable interest. After all, there are safety regulations, inspectors, claims for damages, and so forth. No management is unaware of its duty to avoid accidents or physical conditions which impair workers' health. But workers' brains, minds, and souls are a different matter.

A recent semiofficial report, submitted by the British government to the Stockholm Conference, bears the title "Natural Resources: Sinews for Survival." The most important of all resources are obviously the initiative, imagination, and brainpower of man himself. We all know this and are ready to devote very substantial funds to what we call education. So, if the problem is "survival," one might fairly expect to find some discussion relating to the preservation and, if possible, the development of the most precious of all natural resources, human brains. However, such expectations are not fulfilled. "Sinews for Survival" deals with all the material factors—minerals, energy, water, etc.—but not at all with such immaterial resources as initiative, imagination, and brainpower.

Considering the centrality of work in human life, one might have expected that every textbook on economics, sociology, politics, and related subjects would present a theory of work as one of the indispensable foundation stones for all further expositions. After all, it is work which occupies most of the energies of the human race, and what people actually *do* is normally more important, for understanding them, than what they say, or what they spend their money on, or what they own, or how they vote. A person's work is undoubtedly one of the most decisive formative influences on his character and personality. However, the truth of the matter is that we look in vain for any presentations of theories of work in these textbooks. The question of *what the work does to the worker* is hardly ever asked, not to mention the question of whether the real task might not be to adapt the work to the needs of the worker rather than to demand that the worker adapt himself to the needs of the work—which means, of course, primarily to the needs of the machine.

Let us ask then: How does work relate to the end and purpose of man's being? It has been recognized in all authentic teachings of mankind that every human being born into this world has to work not merely to keep himself alive but to strive toward perfection. To keep himself alive, he needs various goods and services, which will not be forthcoming without human labor. To perfect himself, he needs purposeful activity in accordance with the injunction: "Whichever gift each of you have received, use it in service to one another, like good stewards dispensing the grace of God in its varied forms." From this, we may derive the three purposes of human work as follows:

First, to provide necessary and useful goods and services.

Second, to enable every one of us to use and thereby perfect our gifts like good stewards.

Third, to do so in service to, and in cooperation with, others, so as to liberate ourselves from our inborn egocentricity.

This threefold function makes work so central to human life that it is truly impossible to conceive of life at the human level without work. "Without work, all life goes rotten," said Albert Camus, "but when work is soulless, life stifles and dies."

1. The End of an Era

You can go on and on blowing air into a balloon. The balloon then becomes bigger and bigger, and more and more impressive.

Historians can record with pride and satisfaction the dates when the first efficient pump was invented, and then ever more efficient pumps, and marvelous new chemicals which increased the stretchability of the balloon, and when the balloon reached a certain size, and then twice that size, and how "doubling times" became shorter and shorter and so on.

All these will be important and interesting dates. But none so important and interesting as the date when a hole appeared in the skin of the balloon—perhaps, to start with, quite a small hole—and the air started whistling out.

That date was October 6, 1973.

Things will never be the same again.

I was sitting on a train the other day in England and found myself in a compartment with three gentlemen who were having a heated debate. I couldn't help hearing what they were saying, and I gathered that one of them was a surgeon, one was an architect, and the third was an economist. They were discussing whose was the oldest profession. After a totally inconclusive debate finally the surgeon said, "Look here, come off it! I mean, there's no doubt: if you know Genesis, the Lord took a rib out of Adam to make Eve, and that was a surgical operation."

But, unabashed, the architect said, "Well, long before He did this He had created the whole universe out of chaos: that was an architectural job."

And the economist said merely, "And who created chaos?"

The subject must be seen in this light, particularly now that we have passed the 6th of October, 1973, a date unique in the history of the Western world, a sort of watershed. You will recall that the 6th of October, 1973, was the day when the fourth Arab-Israeli War started. Let's go back into the history, not of this particular war, which merely triggered a situation, but to the history of the situation itself.

As far as my own observations go, after the Second World War there was a general scarcity of fuels, particularly in Europe: everybody was shouting for more coal. And in the middle 1950s the OECD, that organization of the wealthy countries, set up an energy commission which issued a report, *Europe's Energy Requirements: Can They Be Met?* The report said, For goodness' sake, be careful; pull out all stops to work for fuel efficiency; don't neglect Europe's one major energy source, the coal industry. (It also said a few things in ignorance about nuclear energy, as if that might be a savior.) This report was accepted universally as being realistic and truthful. In Britain we set up the National Industrial Fuel Efficiency Service to go through industry and see where fuel could be saved.

And then came the first Suez crisis, about the Suez Canal, and a shock went through all the oil-importing countries, including the United States, the biggest oil producer but also by far the biggest oil consumer. At that time the President of the United States was a former general, General Eisenhower; and he said, What is this? Are we dependent on oil from the Middle East? How so? Well, it was quite easy. America had been extremely richly endowed with oil, but had been exploiting this for a hundred years, and it was now necessary to go deeper and deeper to find the oil. Whereas the Middle East was a relatively new bunch of oil fields, where virtually every bore hole had oil in it. So Middle Eastern oil was very much cheaper than U.S. oil, and more and more Middle Eastern oil was flowing into the United States. And also the oil companies had geared themselves up for this flow.

But Eisenhower looked at it and said, I'm not having it. I'm spending so many billions on armaments, none of which can function without oil, and we're making ourselves dependent on Middle Eastern oil, right next door to the Soviet Union, and the Russian bear with one move of its paw can wipe it out, and what then? So he imposed an import control. If I may say so, the United States is always for free trade except when it doesn't suit her. In this case it didn't suit America to have free trade, so she put on an import control providing, roughly speaking, that 88 percent of American oil requirements would be met from indigenous sources, only 12 percent imported, and that 12 percent primarily from the Western Hemisphere, which means North and South America.

The oil companies, having geared themselves for an ever-increasing flow of oil into the world's biggest market, the United States, found that the shutters had come down. They diverted this oil into Europe, the second-biggest market, and there ensued a murderous competition against coal to make room for the oil, and also internecine, murderous competition between the oil companies to obtain ever-increasing market shares. A part of commercial thinking is not that you're interested in the quantity you sell but in the share of the market. And this murderous competition, against both coal and against each other, induced them to lower prices, and for long periods they were selling at a loss to Europe, just to conquer the market. And of course once the coal mines are shut, you can't reopen them—not deep mines.

One of the sufferers in this was the oil-importing countries, since the price of oil was pressed down and down. And when the companies put the price of oil down again, vis-à-vis the oil-exporting countries, these countries said, We've had enough; we must get together and fight this in self-defense. That was in 1960, when they set up OPEC. Everybody said, Oh, these are Arabs and others, they can't agree with one another, so it's just an attempt to form a cartel and nothing will come of it. Well, of course, for a number of years nothing *did* come of it, because these things have to find their feet, and that takes some time. But they assembled a few knowledgeable people around them—they had all the money in the world to do so—and by the middle 1960s they understood the business.

Previously the oil-exporting countries had nothing to do with their business because it was run by the oil companies, which had immense resources and could assemble a great deal of talent. But now OPEC was assembling this talent, and by around 1965 the oil-exporting countries realized what was happening: that oil is actually not produced by man, it is found by men. It's a sort of larder, and you break into the larder and fetch it out: and when you fetch it out it's no longer there. It's different from producing wheat, where you can produce one crop one year and the next year another crop. And, provided your farming methods are not utterly atrocious, you can go on and on and on doing it; it's not a diminishing asset. But oil, like coal, is extracted: it is a diminishing asset. The oil-producing countries realized this, and, listening to the projections of requirements made by the European countries, by Japan, and by the United States, they said, Good Lord, this is a sellout! We have another twenty or thirty years, and what then? They started making noises. But some understood it better than others. At that time, the person who was most greedy to increase oil output was the Shah of Iran: he couldn't think beyond the end of his nose. He said, If I produce more oil, I get more money.

Well, the others were getting more and more worried

about their resources, and then at the end of 1969
something happened. In Libya there was a change of
government; Colonel Qaddafi chucked out the old king
and became head of state at the ripe old age of twenty-
eight. He inquired, How long will this oil bonanza last?
The answer he got back? Well, we can only go by proved
reserves; how much more might be found heaven
knows; that's pure speculation. But if you want to know
how long these reserves that we actually know exist will
last, at the established rate of expansion they'll last for
eight years. And if you stabilize the rate of output, then
they'll last for twenty years.

Well then, no doubt Colonel Qaddafi, aged twenty-
eight, said twenty-eight plus twenty . . . and what
then? Back to sand and camels . . . I'm not having it. I
want to have at least sixty years ahead of me.

He went to the companies and asked them not to
increase but to throttle output, only marginally. He was
very ill received, and when he found he couldn't really
get along with the companies, he nationalized them so
that he would have control. The immediate effect of *one*
country *marginally* reducing crude-oil output in 1970
was a *50 percent* increase in the world's level of crude-oil
prices.

A lesson was learned that would never be unlearned
again: namely, that with oil, the less you produce the
richer you become. Because oil is a nonreproducible,
nonrenewable asset of limited duration, and the demand is virtually inelastic—there was just as much
motoring after the petrol prices had gone up 20 percent

as there had been before, and motoring is only the tip of the iceberg of oil consumption. But Colonel Qaddafi had become the world's most hated man, and the other Arabs and oil producers didn't want to get into his position. They felt, The oil-importing countries are a dangerous lot, not unused to violence, and we are nothing. They didn't know what to do. They were getting more and more deeply worried about their reserve position, and the fact that, taking all the oil-exporting countries together, on certain assumptions their life expectancy for the oil was seventeen years, on more favorable assumptions twenty to twenty-five years: which makes no difference. I mean, those are just minutes in the life of a nation.

What can you do? You don't want to imitate Colonel Qaddafi and just forge ahead; you want to tread softly. They sent around the General Secretary of OPEC, and he went to all the oil-importing countries making speeches, saying, Now, please, for goodness' sake, mitigate your requirements. This is a big sellout; and what is to become of us? You may be dreaming about Project Independence or about nuclear energy bailing you out or finding more oil in Alaska or the North Sea or under the North Pole. But in order to get this oil and build the pipelines you will be taking all our oil. Of course you're paying for it; but what's the use of it? If you are bleeding to death and you get paid for it that doesn't postpone death. What is to become of *us*? That's the question. Every speech ended, There are 250,000,000 people: what is to become of them? Their only livelihood is oil;

and in twenty-five years we cannot build up an alternative livelihood. So please, please mitigate your requirements.

Of course, nobody listened. Then came the 6th of October, 1973, when, to the consternation of Washington, D.C., the greatest friend of the United States, King Faisal himself, that reliable, honorable gentleman, said, We are now going to use oil as a political weapon against Israel. As long as this war goes on, we shall reduce oil output by 5 percent—or was it 10 percent?—every month. Panic in the oil-importing countries. At the international oil auctions, the price gets bid up more and more and more; within a few weeks it's up to four times its previous level—and that's after the 50 percent increase of 1970. And, when it had reached that level, the oil-exporting countries said, Now, for the first time, we see what our product is really worth, what the importers are willing to pay for it. Let's make that the official price; and now, of course, oil as a political weapon? Forget it. You can have as much as you like, at this price. . . .

Toward the end of the 1960s, the United States made some forecasts about her oil-import requirements, because, although she is still the biggest oil producer, oil outputs leveled off in 1970-71; they have reached their limit and are reckoned to come down. Yet oil consumption is reckoned to go on rising, and so there is a widening gap. About five years ago it was announced from Washington that in 1985 the United States would wish to buy from the Middle East and North Africa as much oil as those territories had ever produced. Needless to say, that gave a little shock both to Japan and to Western Europe. If America buys all the oil, oh no, no, no, the Arabs will have to double the oil output, and particularly Saudi Arabia, the great friend.

So King Faisal sends his oil minister, Mr. Yamani, to the United States just to say, Well, yes, we can expand our oil output—they weren't thinking much about oil reserves—but how are you going to pay for it? And he was told, Well, you can recycle your funds and buy up American industry. But you may remember a few years ago *Time* magazine had an article about 1985, about the Arabian princes arriving in Detroit as the main shareholders of General Motors, and in other places the main shareholders of IBM and Columbia Broadcasting System: a futuristic picture, which at the time seemed to enchant Mr. Yamani. But when Yamani went back to his King and said, It's wonderful! we're going to become the greatest liberated capitalists there ever were; we shall be owning large parts of American industry. Old King Faisal said, Forget it. We Arabs know how easy it is to expropriate the accursed foreign capitalist; one stroke of the pen by Congress and we're expropriated. And what then? We've lost the oil, and what can we do, send a gunboat over to the United States? No, no . . . the only safe investment for the oil is to leave it in the ground unless you need the cash from producing and selling it.

So we already know that they were not prepared to take long-term investments. After all, they *have* experienced how easy it is to expropriate even powerful people: and they are powerless in any other terms

13

except oil. So, the 6th of October, 1973, triggered this, and my own forecast would be—although these things are very difficult to judge—that in the course of the next ten years or so, perhaps much sooner, the output will come down and down and down, to about 50 percent of what it was. Now, as I said, one can't be sure about these things, but that is the logic of *facts*. That we don't notice it yet is because certain accounts are being filled up; but the international banking system is already *creaking* with what used in the past to be called "hot money," money that hasn't found a permanent home and is being switched madly around. When there is a doubt about the value of the dollar, it rushes from New York to Frankfurt, and if then there is a doubt there, it goes to Tokyo, and then there is some trouble in Japan and it goes to Zurich, and so it rushes about: and of course the banking system can't really cope with it.

But that is just the first filling-up process. Any attempts to spend it are futile: even the most extravagant investment projects, like the subway in Teheran, take many years to implement, so the annual rate of expenditure is always a very limited one. It's just not possible to spend these funds, it's not possible to accommodate them in the sort of short-term deposits that absorb them currently. The oil-exporting countries are not willing to risk long-term investment and then expropriation. They will reduce output. And this means that, including of course the sixfold increase in crude oil prices, this very, very short period in history of cheap and plentiful oil is now over.

Things don't change abruptly, but it's gone over the

top, and the prospects are that from now on we shall have dear and scarce oil. If you accept this conclusion, then you have to ask yourself, During that very short and unique period in world history of cheap and plentiful oil, what happened as a result of the cheapness and plenty of oil? How did it crystallize out in our economic life? All those things that have happened as a direct result of cheap and plentiful oil now will be in great danger, the danger of collapse or disappearance when that economic base gradually is withdrawn.

What has become possible from cheap and plentiful oil, or more generally through cheap and plentiful fossil fuel? There is the modern system of agriculture, which is very highly oil-based. What you eat may be, physiologically speaking, all sorts of different foods: economically speaking, you eat mainly oil. (And most of the foods increasingly taste like it . . .) Of course, this didn't use to be the case. We had farming systems in which the job that is now done by oil was done by the microbes in the ground, and biological or organic farming methods, with proper recycling and rotation and whathaveyou. This proved the basis of man's existence, and still of course is in most parts of the world. But, since very little science had gone into it, it was rather stagnant. We have abandoned that, in the West, and have now a system based on chemicals, artificial fertilizers: so, instead of letting the microbes do the job, we let the Arabs do the job! Instead of a renewable resource, we have substituted a nonrenewable resource. People believe that the modern system of agriculture can feed mankind. Well, if we work this out in terms of energy, in terms of oil, if

15

we attempted to feed something like four billion people on modern agricultural technology, then agriculture alone would utilize and absorb all known oil reserves in less than thirty years—agriculture alone.

Evidently this is not a system for world-wide application, and not a system of permanence: it's a short-term system. Consider phosphate. The main phosphate-exporting country is Morocco; and the Moroccans, like the oil-producing countries, have suddenly waked up and seen that this is a nonrenewable asset. Their phosphate deposits are also being exploited at increasing rates, and they can see the end within thirty years or so. The United States has its own phosphate deposits; whether I am rightly informed or not I don't know, but I hear they have made a major contract to export phosphate to the Soviet Union. If that is true, then you are past praying for, because this is one of the real bottlenecks in the agricultural situation on the basis of present modern agricultural technology. So it's not only oil; the whole *problématique* is now coming up with all basic nonrenewable resources except those, like sand, that are everywhere.

In other words, our task now is to rethink the whole situation. If we rethink agriculture, it is no longer permissible to say simply, This system is oil-dependent, but it works! To go about like that is to pretend to ourselves that the present system is in no way threatened and can continue forever and ever. But it can't. It's not a matter of choice; it's a matter of *must*. We must find a more organic system. We don't even have to argue for the more organic system in ecological or in nutritional terms; that is a sort of super-additive to our argument. This system is necessary whether you like it or not.

Another consequence of the short period of cheap and plentiful oil, of course, is the monster cities of today. We say to ourselves, Well, man needs a city; culture cannot arise out of subsistence farming; there has to be a sort of critical density of people to make mutual fertilization possible and produce the flowering of the human spirit. Cities have existed for five or six thousand years; but they could never grow beyond a very modest size. Why not? Because a big city doesn't live on itself, it lives on the land, it lives *off* the land. An inland city lives off the circle of land around it to be provisioned; and in the past that circle couldn't be very large, because the only transport energy was animal and man. Of course, a city situated by the sea could use one other transport energy, namely wind power, and therefore the biggest cities grew up on the seashore, where they could be provisioned by ships. And so we know of no city, until about a hundred years ago, that grew beyond something like two hundred or three hundred thousand people.

Then this bottleneck of how to provision a city was broken by man exploiting fossil fuels, first coal, then oil, and developing a transport technology to use them, so that big cities could be provisioned from all over the world: the hinterland, as it were, of the city became the world. There was one limit to the growth of cities: if it takes eighty people to feed a hundred, then 80 percent of the people must stay on the land and only 20 percent can live in the cities. But, if there is a tremendous increase in the productivity per man—and in this context "man" embraces "woman"—so that five people can feed a hundred, then 95 percent of the people can live in cities and only 5 percent have to stay on the land. So the second precondition was the immense increase in the productivity per man in agriculture, which made the modern city possible.

The city itself is a huge machine which for its very breathing requires a constant, continuous input of energy, namely oil. What is to become of these cities? Even the fourfold increase of fuel prices is making city life more and more onerous and burdensome than it has ever been before. There is no use in referring cities to what we now have learned to call "income energies," like solar power, wind power, etc., because, while you can heat a house with solar energy very comfortably, you can't heat Rockefeller Center. In fact, solar energy plus wind power would not push the lifts up and down. And most of the accommodation in Rockefeller Center is inaccessible if there are no lifts: fancy someone climbing thirty or fifty floors. That is what I mean by life becoming more and more burdensome.

So one has to foresee people leaving the cities and wanting to make a livelihood outside of the cities. Who can receive them? What economic systems are there into which they can escape? They can drop out of the cities, but what can they drop into?

Let's look at transport. The kind of transport that we are used to, of course, is thinkable only on the basis of cheap and plentiful oil. If you go to Detroit you will find a lot of Japanese cars flitting about—evidently, transport is cheap enough to get the car from Tokyo to Detroit and still be able to compete with cars *made* in Detroit. We in England also have Japanese cars; they are just taken as a symbol. When you travel up the big motor road from London you find yourself surrounded by a huge fleet of lorries carrying biscuits from London to Glasgow. And when you look across to the other motorway, you find an equally huge fleet of lorries carrying biscuits from Glasgow to London. Any impartial observer from another planet would come to the inescapable conclusion that biscuits have to be transported at least six hundred miles before they reach their proper quality.

Why is this? Businessmen are not fools; in some sense it pays them to do so. How can it pay them? Of course, cheap and plentiful oil makes it easy; but there is something more behind it. Even a humble article like biscuits is produced in very large outfits, both in London and in Glasgow, which have a very high level of overhead costs. When you have a high level of overhead costs, then the marginal costs—the last packet of biscuits—are very cheap, because the whole caboodle has already been paid for by the other output. Just like, if you have a private boarding school, the first fifty boys pay for the teachers and the buildings and so on and so forth: and the proprietor makes money only off boys number fifty-one and fifty-two. So the marginal costs are a small fraction of the average cost.

Now, the chap in London says, I sell locally what I can sell, but that doesn't fully load up my capacity. And, in order to get it fully loaded up, the marginal costs are only a small fraction. So I can let my marginal product travel long distances—to Glasgow. Even if the transport costs absorb most of the difference between marginal cost and average cost, as long as there is something left it's profitable for me to do so. And he's quite right. Except that the Glasgow chap thinks the same, and he, in order to fill up his capacity, invades the London market. And so, while it is logical from the point of view of the one manufacturer in London and the one manufacturer in Glasgow, if you add it all together it's a total absurdity.

This is the fascination of economics, that there is a logic for business which in terms of the total sum can become an absurdity. That's what makes the subject interesting. But what I want to draw attention to is that this arises out of the *large-scale* production of these biscuits, and the large capitalization. As long as the mode of production is such that marginal costs are only a small fraction of average costs, you will get these phenomena, even with increased transport costs. It is one of the reasons, among many others, that I have reached the conclusion that large-scale production, all issuing from one unit, is also a phenomenon due to cheap and plentiful oil, and is being brought into question as that period of cheap and plentiful oil draws to a close.

What would have to take its place? Instead of large-scale, highly complex and highly capital-intensive production, let's see whether we can't have small units that *ipso facto* wouldn't be so complex. But we would also try to find a much more simplified technology, and it wouldn't require such enormous accumulations of capital.

This would be a very different life-style. We have all been brainwashed by the experience of the nineteenth century, when, probably, the technological immaturity was such that it was true to say, "The bigger the better": only on a large scale can you get the economics of scale. But that was a very immature technology. Now this is no longer true. Today we have enough technological and scientific knowledge to make things small again. This is not a theoretical argument; it cannot be refuted or supported in terms of theory; it's just a matter of getting some people to make the necessary design studies. It may not be true in every field: I don't suppose that one could produce Boeing aircraft on a small scale. But let's begin with basic human requirements. And there I can't see anything that man really *needs* that cannot be produced very simply, very efficiently, very viably on a small scale with a radically simplified technology, with very little initial capital, so that even little people can get at it.

If you have a technological trend, as we've had for the last hundred years, for everything to become bigger and bigger, more and more complex, more and more capital-demanding, then of course more and more people get excluded. The thing is reserved for people already rich or powerful. Have the rich and powerful provided a slot into which the little chaps can fit? Some don't accept the First Commandment, "Thou shalt adapt yourself to slots"; they say, I want to do my own thing, I've got ability and brains and hands, and I want to make something—and then you find you can't, because you haven't got the capital that is needed. The technology has grown beyond the human scale. The question is, Can we bring it back to the human scale? This cannot be asserted or refuted on theoretical grounds, but only on the grounds of practical experience.

We have been at this, with an organization called the Intermediate Technology Development Group, for ten years. And wherever we have tried, we have found, yes, of course, it's perfectly possible. If we want to make cement—although the trend of the cement industry has been to go from small to ever, ever bigger, and now there are installations where half a million tons of cement a year are produced from one factory—if we use the knowhow that we have and make the design study, we can have a mini-plant. And, instead of having one whopper plant in one place, making half a million, we can have a hundred plants scattered around, where the resources are and where the demand is, to make a few thousand tons a year each. This can be done; it can also be done with bricks, it can be done with chipboard, it can be done wherever we've tried. It can be done.

2. Toward a Human-Scale Technology

What is the nature, what are the characteristics of this our actual, present-day industrial society? Everything has a many-sided nature and many characteristics; by what standards are we going to distinguish the essential from the nonessential? If I try to do this "in the light of the Gospel," I must first define how the light of the Gospel appears to me.

First of all, it seems to me, the Gospels tell us that life is a school, a training ground, and cannot therefore be understood simply in its own terms. The Great Headmaster's idea seems to be that we should not merely be comfortable (although comfort as such is not to be despised) but should learn something, strive after something, and with His help become something more than we are. This something is generally called "the Kingdom of Heaven," and the method of attaining it is described as loving God and loving our neighbor as ourselves. But the whole essence of the education is that it should proceed in freedom, that the end product should be persons and not puppets.

I shall therefore try to consider the characteristics of industrial society from the point of view of this all-important task.

Before I do so, I feel I should remind myself of at least one of the great parables in the Gospels, the parable of the wheat and the tares. It suggests that it is part of the great design that they are allowed to grow up together. If we take this seriously, we must expect to encounter the coexistence, almost inextricably inter-mixed, of great good and great evil in our society. For the indications—the signs of the times—are that the season is now pretty far advanced and the time of the harvest, when the wheat will be separated from the tares, may not be far off.

What indications? What signs of the times?

I think there are many, of which I shall mention only one: the extraordinary increase in the rate of change. If you would draw a curve of the rate of change, it would appear as an exponential, or logarithmic, curve of continuous acceleration. It is quite clear that no such curve can proceed for any length of time on this earth. It must come to a stop before long, and that must mean the end of an era and "the revaluation of all values" or, in the imagery of the Gospels, the separation of the wheat from the tares.

Looking at present-day industrial society I should expect therefore to find, inextricably intermixed, great good and great evil. Very likely it is mainly a matter of temperament which of the two impresses you most. But any view or description that includes only the one or the other would be likely to miss an important part of the truth.

Modern industrial society is immensely complicated, immensely involved, making immense claims on man's time and attention. This, I think, must be accounted its greatest evil. Paradoxical as it may seem, modern industrial society, in spite of an incredible proliferation of labor-saving devices, has not given people more time to devote to their all-important spiritual tasks; it has made it exceedingly difficult for anyone, except the most determined, to find any time whatever for these tasks. In fact, I think I should not go far wrong if I asserted that the amount of genuine leisure available in a society is generally in inverse proportion to the amount of labor-saving machinery it employs. If you would travel, as I have done, from England to the United States and on to a country like Burma, you would not fail to see the truth of this assertion. What is the explanation of the paradox? It is simply that, *unless there are conscious efforts to the contrary,* wants will always rise faster than the ability to meet them.

The widespread substitution of mental strain for physical strain is no advantage from our point of view. Proper physical work, even if strenuous, does not absorb a great deal of the power of attention, but mental work does; so that there is no attention left over for the spiritual things that really matter. It is obviously much easier for a hard-working peasant to keep his mind attuned to the divine than for a strained office worker.

I say, therefore, that it is a great evil—perhaps the greatest evil—of modern industrial society that, through its immensely involved nature, it imposes an undue nervous strain and absorbs an undue proportion of man's attention. Of course, it might be otherwise. It is still conceivable, for instance, that hitherto undeveloped countries might pick and choose what they wish to take over from Western industrialism, adopting only those things which really facilitate and enrich life while rejecting all the frills and harmful elaborations. But there is no sign of this happening anywhere in the world. On the contrary, it is cinemas, transistor sets, airplanes and such like which catch on much more quickly than anything really worthwhile.

Whether the tendency to raise wants faster than the ability to meet them is inherent in industrialism as such or in the social form it has taken in the West may be a debatable question. It is certain that it exists and that the social forms exacerbate it. Industry declares that advertising is absolutely necessary to create a mass market, to permit efficient mass production. But what is the great bulk of advertising other than the stimulation of greed, envy, and avarice? It cannot be denied that industrialism, certainly in its capitalist form, openly employs these human failings—at least three of the seven deadly sins—as its very motive force. From the point of view of the Gospels, this must be accounted the very work of the devil. Communism, which rejects and derides the Gospels, does not appear to be bringing forth anything better; its main claim is that it will shortly "overtake" (as they say) Britain or even America. British socialism once upon a time showed an awareness of this evil, which it attributed solely to the peculiar working of the private-enterprise-and-profit system. But today, I am afraid, British socialism has lost its bearings and presents itself merely as a device to raise the standard of living of the less affluent classes faster than could be done by private enterprise. However that may be, present-day industrial society everywhere shows this evil characteristic of incessantly stimulating greed, envy, and avarice. It has produced a folklore of incentives which magnifies individual egotism in direct opposition to the teachings of the Gospel.

R. H. Tawney, one of the great ethical thinkers of our time, has spoken of "the straightforward hatred of a system which stunts personality and corrupts human relations by permitting the use of man by man as an instrument of pecuniary gain." The "system" he refers to is again our modern industrial society, and again it may be a debatable issue whether these evils are the result of industrialism as such or of the particular capitalist form in which it made its appearance in the West. I myself fear it is industrialism as such, irrespective of the social form. In what way does it stunt personality? Whatever Mr. Tawney may have had in mind, I should say: mainly by making most forms of work—manual and white-collared—utterly uninteresting and meaningless. Mechanical, artificial, divorced from nature, utilizing only the smallest part of man's potential capabilities, it sentences the great majority of workers to spending their working lives in a way which contains no worthy challenge, no stimulus to self-perfection, no chance of development, no element of Beauty, Truth, or Goodness. The basic aim of modern industrialism is not to make work satisfying but to raise productivity; its proudest achievement is labor saving, whereby labor is stamped with the mark of undesirability. But what is undesirable cannot confer dignity;

so the working life of a laborer is a life without dignity. The result, not surprisingly, is a spirit of sullen irresponsibility which refuses to be mollified by higher wage awards but is often only stimulated by them.

In addition, industrial society, no matter how democratic in its political institutions, is autocratic in its methods of management. If the workers themselves were given more say in the organization of their work, they might be able to restore some interest and dignity to their daily tasks—but I doubt that they would. After all, they too, like everybody else, are members of modern industrial society and conditioned by the distorted scheme of values that pervades it. How should they know how to do things differently? It is a frequent experience that as soon as a workingman finds himself saddled with managerial responsibility he begins to develop an almost uncanny understanding for and sympathy with the current preoccupations of management. How, indeed, could it be otherwise? Modern industrialism has produced its own coherent system of values, criteria, measurements, etc.; it all hangs together and cannot be tampered with except at the risk of breakdown. If anyone said: "I reject the idolatry of productivity; I am going to ensure that every job is worthy of a man," he would have reason to fear that he might be unable to pay the expected wages or, if he did, that it would land him in the bankruptcy court. All the same, autocratic management, which treats men as "factors of production" instead of responsible human persons, is a grave evil leading to innumerable stunted or even wasted lives.

Maybe a type of industrial society could be developed which was organized in much smaller units, with an almost infinite decentralization of authority and responsibility. From the point of view of the Gospels, a hierarchical structure, i.e., authority as such, is not an evil. But it must be of a size compatible, so to say, with the size of the human being. Structures made up of, say, a hundred people can still be fully democratic without falling into disorder. But structures employing many hundreds or even thousands of people cannot possibly preserve order without authoritarianism, no matter how great the wish for democracy might be.

There are four main characteristics of modern industrial society which, in the light of the Gospels, must be accounted four great and grievous evils:

1. Its vastly complicated nature.
2. Its continuous stimulation of, and reliance on, the deadly sins of greed, envy, and avarice.
3. Its destruction of the content and dignity of most forms of work.
4. Its authoritarian character, owing to organization in excessively large units.

All these evils are, I think, exacerbated by the fact that the bulk of industry is carried on for the purpose of private pecuniary gain. And, although some big business has civilized itself in recent years to a significant extent—largely owing to the "countervailing power" of the trade unions, in conditions of full employment—there still remains a large fringe of big and small business which manifests the worst features of capitalist irresponsibility in an extreme manner. Perhaps the outstanding examples are to be found in the field of communication media—in sections of the press, the entertainment industries, book publishing, and so forth. You may have read Richard Hoggart's *The Uses of Literacy,* which is a terrible indictment. The worst exploitation practiced today is "cultural exploitation," namely, the exploitation by unscrupulous moneymakers of the deep longing for culture on the part of the less privileged and undereducated groups in our society. The exhibition of reading matter on most of the bookstalls in industrial localities is—to my mind—the worst indictment of present-day industrial society. To claim that "this is what the people want" is merely adding insult to injury. It is not what they want, but what they are being tempted to demand by some of their fellow men, who will commit any crime of degradation to make a dishonest penny.

These great and blatant evils are not on the decrease. On the contrary, they are spreading right across the world and all the time gaining in intensity. The modern industrial system has a built-in tendency to grow; it cannot really work unless it is growing. The word "stability" has been struck from its dictionary and replaced by "stagnation." Its continuous growth pursues no particular aims or objectives; it is growth for the sake of growing. No one even inquires after its final shape. There is none; there is no "saturation point." Who, it may be asked, calls the tune? Fundamentally, the technologist. Whatever becomes technologically possible—within certain economic limits—must be done. Society must adapt itself to it. The question whether or not it does any good is ruled out on the specious argument that no one knows anyhow what is good or evil, wholesome or unwholesome, worthy of man or unworthy.

Professor A. Hill says in his book *The Ethical Dilemma of Science:* "To imagine that scientific and technical progress alone can solve all the problems that beset mankind is to believe in magic, and magic of the very unattractive kind that denies a place to the human spirit." What I wish to emphasize is that the modern industrial system does in fact just this and is effectively denying a place to the human spirit. Too much contact with machinery has convinced the masters of the system that economic development is a mechanical, i.e., unalterable, process which could only be thrown into disorder but never stopped or modified by the intrusion of value judgments.

In the face of this preponderance of evil, it may well be asked where one could hope to find even the smallest good. Have not the tares altogether suffocated the wheat?

As a Christian, I am not supposed to fall for the temptation of thinking so. It is the task and function of the devil to do the work of God. There must be some good in these processes, or else why should they be permitted to take place?

You will not expect me now to point to the external, temporal achievements of industrial society as the great good that has grown up alongside the evil. If I did so, I should be guilty of altogether forgetting the great warning in the Gospels: "What shall it profit a man if he shall gain the whole world and lose his own soul?" In the light of the Gospel we cannot but judge that these achievements profit us nothing because they are being purchased by throwing away the pearl of great price. If there is any good to be found, it must be a spiritual good. And I think it is not too difficult to find it.

We can note the gradual spread and establishment of certain basic notions of justice and freedom. Even the greatest evildoers find that they have to justify themselves hypocritically, and "hypocrisy"—as the Duc de la Rochefoucauld observed three hundred years ago—"is the homage paid by vice to virtue." Do not fail to notice the significance of all tyrannies today describing themselves as democracies, and all conquests as liberations, and all arbitrariness as the people's justice. This already is a great victory of light over darkness and a great step forward from the Machiavellian approval of every kind of political crime.

If life is a "school of becoming," a school of self-development, the ideas of personal freedom and personal responsibility must become ever more firmly established. It may be utopian to hope that they will ever gain universal mastery on this earth—because good and evil tend to grow together; but, *as ideas,* they can and, I am sure, will become so powerful that ever greater forces will need to be mobilized by the evil one to resist them. In the ages of slavery, serfdom, and capitalist exploitation at its worst, great masses of people never looked upon themselves as potentially free and responsible. It is different today, even in concentration camps, forced-labor camps, and the like. The average factory worker may make precious little use—or even very damaging use—of his freedom, but he is in no doubt that he has it and that it is a precious thing. No matter how much these ideas are being sinned against, there can be no doubt, I suggest, that, as ideas, they are today more firmly established than ever before. It is ideas that matter more than facts. It is not so long ago that ideas like colonialism, imperialism, "masters and men," and the like seemed perfectly reasonable; they do not any more. Many people, indeed, still argue against the practicability of freedom, of ensuring the dignity of the person, of self-determination, and so forth, but no one argues against the ideas as such.

All this is clearly visible when we look at the modern industrial system. It is indeed authoritarian and may become more so as the size of units increases. But neither the masters nor the men are any more taken in by authoritarianism. The masters are authoritarians with a bad conscience; the men accept them only sullenly and only when they must. There are everywhere discussions on the social obligations of business. People realize that a firm is responsible not only to its shareholders but also to its employees, its customers, and the community as a whole. In Britain, we have a substantial public sector, in which determined efforts are being made to do justice to all, and institutional means have been devised to this end. There are no shareholders; but the employees demand "accountability" through joint consultation, the customers through consumers' councils, and the community through Parliament and the responsible minister.

From my point of view, it is not of decisive importance whether these arrangements *work* "better" or "worse" than undemocratic enterprise; they *are* better, because they are more in line with the meaning of human life than any wealth-producing machine—however successful—that is based upon and motivated by the acquisitive instinct.

Let us return to the thought that life is a school. As one advances in school the tasks and examinations become more difficult. But the problems set by the Great Schoolmaster also become more meaningful and more to the point. Modern industry, by producing comfort on a scale unheard of in human history yet almost destroying the real educational function of daily work, quite clearly sets the most difficult examination task: how not to lose sight of the spiritual in face of these overwhelming temptations. Many people—albeit a small minority—are rising to this task. I think we are living in an age of increasing polarization. A great mass of gray is being separated out into some very black and some very white units. As one might expect, the process seems most advanced in the United States; very great evils are coming all the time from over there (and we, in Europe, strive exceedingly hard to copy and adopt them). But make no mistake: there is also a great drive toward, and consciousness of, goodness in that turbulent society, more plain goodness, I think, than in Europe.

It is my personal belief that, *speaking from a worldly*

point of view, industrial society, unless radically re-formed, must come to a bad end. Now that it has adopted cumulative growth as its principal aim, its end cannot be far off. But that does not mean that it will have failed in its purpose from the point of view of the Gospel. Out of the tremendous examination set by this monstrous development many single individuals will emerge triumphant; uncorrupted and hence incorruptible. This is all that really matters.

This does not mean that we can wash our hands of this worldly failure; for only those can triumph who never cease for a moment, no matter what are the odds against them, to fight evil and try to restore order. "Woe unto the world because of offenses! for it must needs be that offenses come; but woe to that man by whom the offense cometh!" (Matthew 18:7). Anyone who merely "washes his hands" is one of those by whom offense comes.

Why should industrial society fail? Why should the spiritual evils it produces lead to worldly failure? From a severely practical point of view, I should say this:

1. It has disrupted, and continues to disrupt, certain organic relationships in such a manner that world population is growing, apparently irresistibly, beyond the means of subsistence.
2. It is disrupting certain other organic relationships in such a manner as to threaten those means of subsistence themselves, spreading poison, adulterating food, etc.

3. It is rapidly depleting the earth's nonrenewable stocks of scarce mineral resources—mainly fuels and metals.
4. It is degrading the moral and intellectual qualities of man while further developing a highly complicated way of life the smooth continuance of which requires ever-increasing moral and intellectual qualities.
5. It breeds violence—a violence against nature which at any moment can turn into violence against one's fellow men, when there are weapons around which make nonviolence a condition of survival.

It is no longer possible to believe that any political or economic reform, or scientific advance, or technological progress could solve the life-and-death problems of industrial society. They lie too deep, in the heart and soul of every one of us. It is there that the main work of reform has to be done—secretly, unobtrusively. I think we must study nonviolence deep down in our own hearts. It may or may not be right to "ban the bomb." It is more important to overcome the roots out of which the bomb has grown. I think these roots are a violent attitude to God's handiwork instead of a reverent one. The unsurpassable ugliness of industrial society—the mother of the bomb—is a sure sign of its violence. "Blessed are the patient; they shall inherit the land," and "Blessed are the peacemakers; they shall be counted the children of God." (Matthew 5:5,9, Knox translation.)

I shall be asked to declare what any one of us can *do* in this very difficult situation. What did Christians do during the breakdown of the Roman Empire? They did not run away but went to work cheerfully among the apparent doom. The degeneration of the industrial system—that is, its ever-intensified idolatry of getting rich quickly—offers everywhere ample opportunities for bringing light into dark places. Everywhere the values of freedom, responsibility, and human dignity have to be openly affirmed, even where a neglect of these values would appear to allow the big industrial machine to run more smoothly and more efficiently. It may not be possible to do this without causing offense. To tell a young person that his personal integrity is more important than his career may sound almost like sabotage in the ears of the efficiency experts. To insist that the reckless waste of natural resources is a crime does not sound cooperative to those who think that the highest possible rate of consumption is the only worthwhile pursuit for mortal man.

It is the individual, personal example that counts. The greatest "doing" that is open to every one of us, now as always, is to foster and develop within oneself a genuine understanding of the situation which confronts us, and to build conviction, determination, and persuasiveness upon such understanding. Let us face it, to look at modern industry in the light of the Gospels is not the fashion of the day, and the diagnosis I have given here is not acceptable, at this point in time, to the great majority of our contemporaries. What, then, is the use of asking for a "program of action"? Those who have understood know what to do. They also know that, although in a minority, they do not stand alone.

Few people deny that technological change has political consequences; yet equally few people seem to realize that the present "system," in the widest sense, is the product of technology and cannot be significantly changed unless technology is changed.

The question may be asked: What is it that has produced modern technology? Various answers can be given. We may go back to the Renaissance, or even further, to the arising of Nominalism, and point to certain changes in Western man's attitude to religion, science, nature, and society, which then apparently released the intellectual energies for modern technological development. Marx and Engels gave a more direct explanation: the rising power of the bourgeoisie, that is, "the class of modern capitalists, owners of the means of social production, and employers of wage labour."

The bourgeoisie, wherever it has got the upper hand, has put an end to all feudal, patriarchal, idyllic relations. It has pitilessly torn asunder the motley feudal ties that bound man to his "natural superiors," and has left no other bond between man and man than naked self-interest, than callous "cash payment."

It compels all nations, on pain of extinction, to adopt the bourgeois mode of production.

The bourgeoisie has subjected the country to the rule of the towns. It has created enormous cities . . . has agglomerated population, centralized means of production, and has concentrated property in a few hands.

If the bourgeoisie did all this, what enabled it to do so? The answer cannot be in doubt; the creation of modern technologies. Once a process of technological development has been set in motion it proceeds largely by its own momentum, irrespective of the intentions of its originators. It demands an appropriate "system," for inappropriate systems spell inefficiency and failure. Whoever created modern technology, for whatever purpose, this technology or, to use the Marxian term, these modes of production, now demand a system that *suits them,* that is appropriate to them.

As our modern society is unquestionably in crisis, there must be something that does not fit. (a) If overall performance is poor despite brilliant technology, maybe the "system" does not fit. (b) Or maybe the technology itself does not fit present-day realities, including human nature.

Which of the two is it? This is a very crucial question. The assumption most generally met is that the technology is all right—or can be put right at a moment's notice—but that the "system" is so faulty it cannot cope:

Modern bourgeois society with its relations of production, of exchange and of property, a society that has conjured up such gigantic means of production and of exchange, is like the sorcerer who is no longer able to control the powers of the nether world whom he has called up by his spells . . . The conditions of bourgeois society are too narrow to comprise the wealth created by them. And how does the bourgeoisie get over these crises? On the one hand by the enforced destruction of a mass of productive forces; on the other, by the conquest of new markets and by the more thorough exploitation of the old ones. That is to say, by paving the way for more extensive and more destructive crises, and by diminishing the means by which crises are prevented. (Marx and Engels: *Manifesto of the Communist Party*, 1848.)

The culprit is the capitalist system, the profit system, the market system, or, alternatively, nationalization, bureaucracy, democracy, planning, or the incompetence of the bosses. In short: we have a splendid train but a bad track or a rotten driver or a lot of stupid, unruly passengers.

Maybe all this is quite true, except that we do not have such a splendid train at all. Maybe what is most wrong is that which has been and continues to be the strongest formative force—the technology itself.

If our technology has been created mainly by the capitalist system, is it not probable that it bears the marks of its origin, a technology for the few at the expense of the masses, a technology of exploitation, a technology that is class-orientated, undemocratic, inhuman, and also unecological and nonconservationist?

I never cease to be astonished at the docility with which people—even those who call themselves Socialists or Marxists—accept technology uncritically, as if technology were a part of natural law. As an example of this "docility" we may take the Prime Minister of Iran, who is reported to have said in a recent interview (*To the Point International*, January 12, 1976):

There are many aspects of the West that we particularly wish to avoid in the industrialization of Iran. *We seek the West's technology only, not its ideology.* What we wish to avoid is an ideological transplant.

The implicit assumption is that you can have a technological transplant without getting at the same tine an ideological transplant; that technology is ideologically neutral; that you can acquire the hardware without the software that lies behind it, has made the hardware possible, *and keeps it moving.* Is this not a bit like saying: I want to import eggs for hatching, but I don't want chicks from them but mice or kangaroos?

I do not wish to overstate the case; there is nothing absolutely clear-cut in this world and, no doubt, many different tunes can be played on the same piano; but whatever is played, it will be piano music. I agree with the general meaning of Marx's rhetorical question:

Does it require deep intuition to comprehend that man's ideas, views, and conceptions—in a word, man's consciousness—changes [he does not say: is totally determined] with every change in the conditions of his material existence, in his social relations and in his social life?

It is a great error to overlook or to underestimate the effects of the "modes of production" upon people's *lives,* not just their "standard of living":

- how they produce; what they produce;
- where they work; where they live; whom they meet;

41

- how they relax or "recreate" themselves; what they eat, breathe, and see;
- and therefore what they think, their freedom or their dependence.

Adam Smith was under no illusion about the effects of the "mode of production" on the worker:

The understandings of the greater part of men are necessarily formed by their ordinary employments. The man whose whole life is spent in performing a few simple operations . . . has no occasion to exert his understanding . . . He naturally loses, therefore, the habit of such exertion and generally becomes as stupid and ignorant as it is possible for a human creature to become . . . But in every improved and civilized society this is the state into which the labouring poor, that is, the great body of the people, must necessarily fall, unless government takes some pains to prevent it.

Marx comments that "some crippling of body and mind is inseparable even from division of labour in society as a whole. Since, however, manufacture carries this . . . much further and also, by its peculiar division, attacks the individual at the very roots of his life, it is the first to afford the materials for, and give start to, industrial pathology." And he quotes his contemporary, D. Urquhart, who says: "The subdivision of labour is the assassination of a people."

People still say: It is not the technology; it is the "system." Maybe a particular "system" gave birth to this technology; but now it stares us in the face that the system we have is the product, the inevitable product, of the technology. As I compare the societies which appear to have different "systems," the evidence seems to be overwhelming that where they employ the same technology they act very much the same and become more alike every day. Mindless work in office or factory is equally mindless under any system.

I suggest therefore that those who want to promote a *better* society, achieve a *better* system, must not confine their activities to attempts to change the "super-structure"—laws, rules, agreements, taxes, welfare, education, health services, etc. The expenditure incurred in trying to buy a better society can be like pouring money into a bottomless pit. If there is no change in the base—which is technology—there is unlikely to be any *real* change in the superstructure.

People say to me: Before you can make headway with your intermediate technology you must first change the system, do away with capitalism and the profit motive, dissolve the multinationals, abolish all bureaucracies, and reform education. All I can reply is: I know of no better way of changing the "system" than by putting into the world a *new type* of technology—technologies by which small people can make themselves productive and relatively independent.

Or is there a better way? If so, let's have it. Expansion of nationalization, welfare, redistributive taxation? Local government reform? Changes in political representation? Planning? Yes, all these things have their points, and we have had plenty of them, and the more things change the more they remain the same, unless they get worse.

During the eighteenth and nineteenth centuries technology just grew like Topsy. Increasingly, however, it became the outgrowth of science. Today, its primary derivation is from science; in fact, it appears that science is today mainly valued for its technological fruits.

Starting, then, with science, the question may be raised: What determines the course of science? There is always more that *could* be studied than *can* be studied; so there is need for choice, and how is it made?

By the interests of scientists? Yes, unquestionably.

By the interests of big business and government? Surely yes.

By the interests of "the people"? On the whole, no!

The people have fairly simple requirements to meet for which hardly any additional science is needed. (It could be that an entirely different *kind* of science would really benefit the people; but that is another matter.)

Moving on from science to technology, there is again far more that *could* be done than *can* be done. The choice is endless. Who decides or what decides? Scientific findings can be used for, incarnated in, countless different shapes of technology, but new technologies are developed only when people of power and wealth back the development. In other words, the new technologies will be in the image of the system that brings them forth, *and they will reinforce the system*. If the system is ruled by giant enterprises—whether privately or publicly owned—the new technologies will tend to be "gigantic" in one way or another, designed for "massive breakthroughs," at massive cost, demanding extreme specialization, promising a massive impact—no matter how violent—"we shall know how to cope with the consequences." The slogan is "A breakthrough a day keeps the crisis at bay." We hear of "white hot technological revolution," the Nuclear Age, the Age of Automation, the Space Age, fantastic feats of engineering, supersonic triumphs, all that; but many of the most basic needs of great masses of people, such as housing, cannot be taken care of.

The most telling example, of course, is the most advanced society of the modern world, the United States. Average income per head is over twice that of Britain or Western Europe, and yet there is more degrading poverty in the States than you can ever see in Europe; 5 or 6 percent of the world population using something like 35 percent of the world's output of raw materials—and not a happy place: great wealth in some places but utter misery, degradation, hopelessness, strife, criminality, escapism, sickness of body and mind almost everywhere; it is hard to get away from it. How is it possible—in a country that has more resources, more science and technology than anybody ever had in human history? People are questioning everything, every part of the superstructure—big business, big government, big academia; and very gradually, hesitantly, at long last they are beginning to question the basis of it all—technology.

Technology assessment groups have sprung up in various places; they "assess" technological developments mainly in the light of three questions:

What does it do in terms of resource usage?
What does it do to the environment?
What is its socio-political relevance?

45

Concorde did not fare well under their scrutiny. They concluded that it was wasteful of scarce resources, environmentally burdensome and even dangerous, and socio-politically irrelevant. It may nonetheless be described as a marvelous achievement of Anglo-French engineering.

Let us follow through a few of the structural effects of modern technology. Its effect on the nature of work has already been referred to. It is, I believe, the greatest destructive force in modern society. What could be more destructive than the destruction of people's understanding? Matters have not improved since Adam Smith's time; on the contrary, the relentless elimination of creative work for the great majority of the population has proceeded apace.

What has been the effect of modern technology upon the *pattern of human settlement*? This is a very interesting subject which has received hardly any attention. The UN and the World Bank produce indices of urbanization, showing the percentage of the population of different countries living in urban areas (above a certain size). The interesting point is that these indices entirely miss the interesting point. Not the degree but the *pattern* of urbanization is the crux of the matter. Human life, to be fully human, needs the city; but it also needs food and other raw materials gained from the country. Everybody needs ready access to both countryside and city. It follows that the aim must be a *pattern* of urbanization so that every rural area has a nearby city, near enough so that people can visit it and be back the same day. No other pattern makes human sense.

Actual developments during the last hundred years or so, however, have been in the exactly opposite direction: the rural areas have been increasingly deprived of access to worthwhile cities. There has been a monstrous and highly pathological polarization of the pattern of settlements. The French planners fight against France becoming "Paris surrounded by a desert," in the United States they have coined the term "megalopolis" to describe the vast conurbations which have arisen while the life has been seeping out of small and medium-sized country towns. There is Boswash extending from Boston to Washington, D.C.; there is Chicpitts, a conurbation stretching from Chicago to Pittsburgh; and there is Sansan, from San Francisco to San Diego. Even in the United Kingdom, often referred to as a tightly packed little island, the pattern of settlement is extraordinarily lopsided, with more than half the area grossly underpopulated and large parts of the other half madly congested.

Do you remember this socialist demand, formulated more than one hundred years ago?

Combination of agriculture with manufacturing industries; gradual abolition of the distinction between town and country by a more equable distribution of the population over the country. (*Communist Manifesto.*)

And what has happened during those more than one hundred years? Of course, the exact opposite. And what is expected to happen during the next twenty-five years, to the end of the century? Again the exact opposite, with a vengeance. Not urbanization but, to use a word as dreadful as the phenomenon it denotes, *megalopolitanization*, a movement that produces, as we know only too well, utterly insoluble political, social, moral, psychological, and economic problems.

A paper issued by the World Bank speaks of

the despondency surrounding the task of ameliorating urban conditions in the developing countries [which] arises primarily from the speed of urban growth and shortage of resources, human as well as financial. . . .
Urban administration is woefully lacking in capacity to deal with the problems. . . .
Yet within less than twenty years the present populations and areas of urban centres will account for less than a third of the total.

The paper asks whether there is a possibility "of accelerating the development of small and medium-size towns or creating new urban growth centres." But it loses little time in dismissing this possibility:

Most small urban centres . . . lack the basic infrastructure of transport and services . . . Management and professional staff are unwilling to move from the major cities.

This tells the whole story: Management and staff are unwilling to move from the major cities! The proposition, evidently, is to transplant into a small place the technology which has been developed in such a way *that it fits only a very large place.* The people in the small place cannot cope with it; management and staff have to be

48

imported from the "major cities," no one wants to come because the proposition does not make economic sense. The technology is inappropriate and that means the whole project is uneconomic.

With a name like mine, I find it easy to understand that to be a good shoemaker it is not enough to know a lot about making shoes; you also have to know about feet. The shoe made for the big fellow does not fit the foot of the little fellow. The small foot needs a different shoe, *not an inferior one* but one of the right size. Modern technology, generally speaking, makes good shoes only for big fellows. It is geared to mass production; it is highly sophisticated and enormously capital-costly. Of course it does not fit anywhere but in or near the biggest cities or megalopolitan areas.

The simple answer to this problem does not seem to have occurred to many people. It is: let us mobilize at least a small part of our intellectual and other resources to create a technology that *does* fit the smaller places.

Incredible amounts of money are being spent in trying to cope with the relentless growth of megalopolitan areas and in trying to infuse new life into "development areas." But if you say, Spend a little bit of money on the creation of technologies that *fit the given conditions of development areas,* people accuse you of wanting to take them back into the Middle Ages.

One thing, however, can be asserted with confidence: unless suitable, appropriate technologies for efficient production *outside* the main conurbations are created, the destructive tendencies of megalopolitanization will continue to operate with all that this implies socially, politically, morally, environmentally, and resource-wise.

Having traced the effect of modern technology upon the nature of work and the pattern of human settlement, let us now consider a third example, a highly political one, its effect on human freedom. This is undoubtedly a tricky subject. What is freedom? Instead of going into long philosophical disquisitions, let us ask the more or less rebellious young what they are looking for.

Their negations are such as these:

I don't want to join the rat race.
Not be enslaved by machines, bureaucracies, boredom, ugliness.
I don't want to become a moron, robot, commuter.
I don't want to become a fragment of a person.

I want to do my own thing.
I want to live (relatively) simply.
I want to deal with people, not masks.
People matter. Nature matters. Beauty matters. Wholeness matters.
I want to be able to *care*.

All this I call a longing for freedom.

Why has so much freedom been lost? Some people say, Nothing has been lost; but people are asking for more than before. Whichever way it is: there is a gap between supply and demand of this most precious thing—freedom. Has technology anything to do with this? The size and complexity of organizations certainly has a great deal to do with it. Why is the trend of the last hundred years toward bigger and bigger units? Nobody, except a few monomaniac tycoons, likes them. Why do we have to have them? The invariable answer is: Because of technological progress.

What we have to do now is not abandon technology, but become conscious of somewhere having taken a wrong turn. Under the influence of fossil fuel at throwaway prices, technology has taken the wrong turn, I suggest, in four directions.

First of all, there is a trend for everything to become bigger and bigger. (We call this quality "economies of scale.") This applies of course on the organizational level, but also on the purely technical level the units become bigger and bigger. The normal and standard size of brickworks in the nineteenth century produced ten thousand bricks a week. By the turn of the century it had risen to a hundred thousand bricks a week; today the standard size is between one and two million bricks a week. And now the Shah of Iran wants a five-million-bricks-a-week brickworks. That is one tendency, toward what I call giantism.

The second tendency is that things are becoming, are *made*, ever more complex. The complexity of equipment, the ingenuity that is invested in quite humble things, is fantastic. I haven't seen it with my own eyes, but I was told that if you really want to be "with it" you should go and buy a tube of toothpaste—you squeeze it, and the toothpaste comes out in three different luscious colors. And it's so clever they don't even get mixed up; it's like a flag coming out . . . three colors. But also, the other day I traveled in a car, and of course the boy who still survives in every man rejoices, because I was not subjected to the indignity of having to turn a handle to wind the window up or down, but I had to press a button. And I had a job to find the other button to get the thing down again!

Why this complexity? This complexity is a kind of disease. Even if it's not a question of cost, you can avoid its being immensely costly only by handing this production over to mindless machines, and mass-production machines. And also, of course, the more complex a thing is the more it tends to break down, and then where are you headed? You can't possibly repair it yourself, it's too complex. So you take it to a garage, and it costs you $150, not to mention how long the car might be immobilized.

I traveled in the winter in Germany with a friend who had a splendid Mercedes, but the electrical system had developed a small fault and all the windows were stuck in different positions. He drove from garage to garage but there was no one who could penetrate the system, and all winter he drove in an icy blast. Finally in the spring he found someone to repair it for $300. Is that a price worth paying so you don't have to turn the handle?

We joke about this but it is an extremely serious matter—that technology, although it was created by man, has become a force of its own; it has shaped man, a vast number of men, into little parrots that twitter and push and scrape to make things more and more complicated. And when they have found something that can actually be done, no matter how futile or dangerous it may be, such as Concorde or nuclear power, then they create a kind of Mafia to see that it gets done.

The third point is connected with the first and second. Things have become so capital-costly that you have to be already rich and powerful before you can really do anything. This is a very serious matter: for instance, to give only one example and not the prime example, take agriculture. You have highly scientific, highly chemicalized farming in very large units, and it is an outstanding fact that, if one wants to live off the land, supplying himself and his family with the wherewithal, he needs to be of quite exceptional industry and intelligence to make a very humble living. All the research has gone in the opposite direction, to ever-greater capital requirements. To start a farm on the established system, even if you believe in the established system, is so capital-intensive that you have to be rich to do it. So more and more people get excluded. This of course hits most massively the poor countries, who find that they can't do most of the things because they are so capital-intensive. An intermediate technology that would not require this capital is not readily available; so they are excluded. Then they are told just to go on buying it from the rich countries. And the fact is, with their developing they are becoming not more independent but more dependent.

The fourth criterion of this technological development I would call violence. When you look at it from this point of view, and widen the concept of violence beyond human warfare, you find—and ecologists have confirmed it—an ever-increasing warfare against nature, and violent attitudes: the belief that science can do everything, and so you can go bullheadedly along, dumping poisons in ever-increasing quantities on this thin film around the globe, on which all life depends. If there are any unwanted side effects, science will deal with them. Or take medicine: the whole direction has been one to increasing violence. I know even from very sad family experience that the number of people who are the victims not of their diseases but of the cures prescribed for them is very great, and the damage done is often totally irreparable. Whereas preventive medicine is still virtually totally neglected. A very clever chap once said that if an ancestor of long ago would visit us today, what would he become astonished at: the skill of our dentists or the rottenness of our teeth? This is a very neat way of putting it; it shows we cannot reject, we have to be grateful for the skill of our dentists, because of the rottenness of our teeth. This is a mutual escalation: our teeth are still more rotten, and we are still more grateful for the dentists. A nonviolent approach to it would put the best of human intelligence into resolving the question Why are our teeth so rotten?

If this is a correct diagnosis of the development of the last hundred years—ever-bigger size, ever-bigger complexity, ever-bigger capital intensity, and ever-bigger violence—then it would seem to follow that the cure must be sought in the opposite direction. But the cure is not found necessarily by going *back,* because in a hundred years, in the only knowledge that can accumulate, namely scientific knowledge, knowledge of dead matter really—there will be a great deal of progress. And things that were not possible to do very easily on a small scale in the nineteenth century we *can* do on a small scale now. But not when the engineers have been brainwashed and educated all their lives in the opposite direction, so they don't believe it. It is possible to make things smaller—I'm not saying in every instance, but as regards all basic human requirements.

Second, it is possible to do many things in a much simpler way. Any third-rate engineer can make a complicated apparatus more complicated, but it takes a touch of genius to find one's way back to the basic principles, which are normally fairly simple. I'm not saying that the good Lord has arranged the world everywhere in a simple manner. No, no, He has distributed quite nicely to keep us alert. We have to use our brains. . . . But certainly not in the way we are doing now. Once we go and get down to work, we find we learn to distinguish what is essential and what are sort of almost cancerous growths, *almost* cancerous. If you think in these terms, and look at modern machine tools, you then learn to distinguish between the *tool* and the machine tool. That, of course, should be the best that human ingenuity can make, and normally it is a very simple thing.

And third, if one realizes that the immense capital requirements *are* a principle of exclusion, are totally incompatible with any ideas of justice or equality, then one will systematically search for cheaper ways of doing things. I mentioned before the little boy in every man; I suppose there is a little boy even in every woman, not only a little girl. There is nothing more beautiful to me than tools; in fact, I always have to restrain myself from buying any number of tools, and have to remind myself that I wouldn't be able to find the time to use them. But I like the feeling of having good tools around—my tools are all kept in my study. . . . That is really intelligence, a tool. A machine? It is perhaps a tool, but it's not a tool operated by man; it's a tool operated by a mindless mechanism. And these mechanisms become bigger and more complex, and more and more attuned to mass production, and then they become immensely expensive.

Henry Ford started the Ford Motor Company with a capital of $30,000. The dollar has gone down in purchasing value, mark it down by whatever you like—mark it down by three, or four, or five, you have $100,000. At a cost of $100,000 you cannot change one *screw* in a modern motorcar. To have a new model now costs $300,000,000 and takes four years of preparation. Who can afford it? I can't.

But, when Ford started, it was uncertain whether the steam engine wasn't better than the petrol engine: he could have switched from a petrol engine to a steam engine in the shortest possible time without disturbing anybody, and for very little money. Can't we look back in that direction? Can't we think more in terms of *tools* and learn to distinguish tools from machines, create facilities for people to become productive who have got it in them to do that which may then turn out to be extremely viable.

And fourth, if the thing has gone in the direction of violence, let's look in the direction of nonviolence. Nonviolence, in this context, refers to modes of production which respect ecological principles and strive to work with nature instead of attempting to force their way through natural systems, in the conviction that unintended damage and unforeseen side effects can always be undone by the further application of violence. All too often one problem is "solved" by creating several new ones. Poor societies cannot afford this kind of violence, and it may indeed be doubted whether the rich societies (or "sectors") can afford it much longer.

These four criteria or "guidelines" for new technological research and development may not appeal to everyone; all that can be said in their favor is that they have arisen out of actual work, not simply out of theorizing. Experience shows that whenever you can achieve smallness, simplicity, capital cheapness, and nonviolence, or, indeed, any one of these objectives, new possibilities are created for people, singly or collectively, to help themselves, and that the patterns that result from such technologies are more humane, more ecological, less dependent on fossil fuels, and closer to real human needs than the patterns (or life-styles) created by technologies that go for giantism, complexity, capital intensity, and violence. It is incumbent on those who reject these criteria or guidelines to come forward with another set; because as long as there are no guidelines the search for alternatives cannot even begin.

Now this is real work. And the sooner we start this work on a systematic basis, the better. I rejoice in the fact that many people are starting, or have been active even for a number of years. But what now needs to be done is to make sure that we, whose strength is very small, don't all reinvent the wheel, that we get into such relationships that we can learn from one another and benefit from each other's experience.

I'll give you an example of real work, of nonviolent technology. I was asked by the President of Zambia to visit his country, and he received me at the state house. There he was sitting with his cabinet and he was holding a sheaf of papers in his hand and introduced me quickly and said, "This is why we have asked you to come, what do we do? I have been stumping the country with our Five Year Plan, I have told everybody this is now the Bible"—and then with a grand gesture he threw the papers on the floor and said, "I now realize it was the wrong Bible."

What is wrong with it? It applies only to the cities around the Copper Belt, and to Lusaka, the capital, while wide rural areas are totally left out. One of the things the Zambian government was particularly interested in was improving nutrition: they don't starve there, but there is a lot of malnutrition because of what they call the "protein gap." To fill the protein gap, they had a slogan: "One egg a day for every Zambian." And they were building up egg production quite successfully. I visited a lot of these farmers, and I found them weeping over their eggs, which were covering the floors of their sheds. "What are you doing with them, are you hatching them, or what?" "No, we haven't got any packaging material to send them to market. The supply of egg trays—which used to come from South Africa, from Britain, from America—has somehow stopped, and we have nothing to do with these eggs. We can't take them to market in our trouser pockets. What are we to do? They are just rotting."

Lighthearted as I normally am, I said, "Well, why don't you make egg trays in Zambia?" Of course, nobody in Zambia knew how to do it, nor did I. Coming back to London, we investigated. We found that virtually all the egg trays in the world are made by one multinational company. We contacted the European branch of this multinational company, and they said, "No problem! I mean, we'll build a factory in Lusaka—how many do they want?" "Well, a rough calculation suggests about a million a year. It's a very small population, right in the beginning of development."

Long pause . . . "Forget it. The smallest machine makes a million a month. So, unless you can somehow organize an All-Africa Common Market for Egg Trays, and build the roads for the lorries all coming out of Lusaka, to distribute the egg trays to the rural areas . . ." I said, "But this is the very opposite of helping people, the opposite of development, just to refer them to foreign trade, to importing stuff. Why don't you make a small plant?" "Oh no, we get many requests for small units, but our engineers say it would be totally uneconomic."

It was no go with them. We got a young fellow and gave him two jobs: first of all to redesign the egg tray, which we considered very badly designed. (The multi-national company does big business, but they don't seem to have a very good designer: when you fill the egg trays and put one on top of the other, the whole thing wobbles, and you still have to crate it to ship it, and crating is very expensive.) This job was taken to the Royal College of Art in London and within six weeks we had the perfect design, a perfectly stable assembly—tie it together with a string, ship it like that, not a single egg gets broken.

The second assignment was more difficult: to create a mini-plant. We did this with the Engineering Department of the University of Reading. It was going back to first principles, the sort of work that any think tank does, not to start from where others have got to. The prototype was built and we found a small manufacturer. That plant has 2 percent of the capacity of the hitherto smallest plant, and 2 percent of the capital cost; and it's totally compatible. And now, what was the reaction of the formidable dinosaur, the multinational company, of whom so many of my young colleagues are terrified? They said, "Well, you know, we want to remain the kings of egg trays—that is our ambition in life. We have agreed that the small scale requirements we cannot meet—couldn't we come to some agreement?" They said, below this line of size it's yours, above that, it's ours. And in return for the privilege that they can remain the kings of egg trays, and not be disturbed by the little princes like myself, they gave us access to some of their knowhow at the most ticklish points in the works, namely the mold which forms the egg tray. A healthy cooperation has developed between the whale and the sardine.

I mention only this case but I could go on for a long time. Nobody should think this is a dream; this is an activity. This is possible. And while I am not suggesting that we could have a simplified technology to land people on the moon, I am suggesting that our experience implies that on all real human requirements that can be the case. And if we don't land people on the moon, I don't think the loss will be overwhelming. (I myself was initially quite in favor of the program and had quite a list of people. But when I found they all had to come back again I couldn't see the point of it.)

These are just a few indications of what I know can be done and needs to be done now. It requires systematic work. I don't think it requires a large part of the resources of a rich society. I would say 95 percent of the research and development people can play their games as before, but 5 percent should be diverted relevant to the future. Not that I would limit it to that, I would be happier if the percentage was greater; I just want to indicate how modest my proposals are. Small amounts are normally more difficult to mobilize than large.

All this is not just a spinning of theories, although everything has to begin by theories. This is now backed up by work, work that has been carried on over ten years and has spread to many places in the world. It has spread also inside the U.K., where people say we need a different technology. This is not a recession. This is an end of an era. There's rising unemployment. These unemployed will not be automatically reabsorbed into these highly capitalized jobs. What is to become of them? While the unemployment rises, the budgetary allocations are cut down. All sorts of needful things are not done. We are not going to go on waiting for Godot, and Godot never comes. In other words, we are not going to go on waiting for the central government. We are going to stand on our own two feet and do within the context of our community what needs doing. This sort of self-remembering is now coming, and people are realizing that in order to make what needs doing efficient and effective one must engage intellectual resources to create an appropriate, suitable technology.

Recently I saw a film of Gandhi when he came to England in 1930. He disembarked in Southampton and on the gangway he was already overwhelmed by journalists asking questions. One of them asked, "Mr. Gandhi, what do you think of modern civilization?" And Mr. Gandhi said, "That would be a good idea." I think now the time has come when we can implement this good idea.

If one actually, consciously engages in work in these four directions—not all four may be feasible all at once—one can also mobilize support from people who are going hell for leather in the opposite direction, because they are all a bit rattled. Of course if one simply says, What you are doing is terrible and you are this or that, and denounces it, then one doesn't get the best cooperation. But one can convince, if not the organizations, at least people in the organizations, that something, some reorientation, is necessary and that they have the resources and they can do it without any strain.

My formula for this is a lifeboat. I have persuaded some big farmers in England to have a lifeboat, to separate out a bit of their land, which they don't need for making a living—they make their living on 95 percent of their land, and take 5 percent and run this as an organic unit or experimental unit to try to minimize their dependence on a very sophisticated and vulnerable industrial system. Well, after some persuasion this is actually happening. They are hard up as to who is going to manage this, because we haven't trained any people in nonchemical methods of farming. And of course it is harder now than it was fifty years ago, because the standardized farming, the chemicals, virtually irrespective of the quality of the soil, has lost us the traditional knowledge. Oh no, for this spot of land you take this and for that you take that, otherwise you get infestation. Why worry about infestation? You've got insecticides. Otherwise you get overrun with weeds. . . . Why worry about that? We've got herbicides, etc. Or this is a poor soil and that is a rich soil—well, why make a distinction? We have chemicals; we don't grow plants out of the soil, we grow them out of chemicals.

With this attitude, this standardization, this unification, the knowledge of how really to cooperate with the soil is very largely lost. It has to be regained. It's much more difficult now but still it can be done.

If we engage in this work and do it intelligently, and are clever enough to engage people who at first sight might be our enemies, then I find it's not going to be very difficult and not going to be all that lengthy. If there were enough people, I think we could have an alternative technology, alternative possibilities, absolutely established over the whole range of basic human requirements. This is a finite job.

But people say, That's all very nice, but really technology, that has nothing to do with it, that's just tinkering. You have to change the system, or you have to change the philosophy, or how do you change human nature, or how do you stop the population growth? There are all sorts of things we *can* do—I mean *we,* now, not in the abstract, as we are also sitting here—and there are other things we can't do. One of the greatest confusions, in most discussions, is the term "we." You know, people say, We ought to decentralize General Motors. I look at them—I couldn't decentralize the drugstore on the corner! Or we ought really to change human nature—they couldn't even change their own nature! When I say "we" I am asking what can actual people, small as they are, what can they do?

If you look at it this way, you find that if one could make visible the possibility of alternatives, viable alternatives, make a viable future already visible in the present, no matter on how small a scale, even if it's only with a Scott Nearing—then at least there is something, and if that something fits, it will be taken. Suddenly there will be demand. If one establishes something, then one gets the benefit that this technology is not simply made by man but it also makes men. A type of technology that is not born out of the system we deplore will create a system we can approve of. If little people can do their own thing again, then perhaps they can do something to defend themselves against the overbearing, big ones.

So I certainly never feel discouraged. I can't myself raise the winds that might blow us, or this ship, into a better world. But I can at least put up the sail so that, when the wind comes, I can catch it.

3. A Viable Future Visible in the Present

It's not useful to talk about capitalism or socialism or nationalization unless one knows what one is talking about. After all, the economy consists of many very different bits and pieces. I have come to the conclusion that where you have lots of small businesses filling all sorts of demands, they do not constitute a social problem. They don't individually have a tremendous impact on the society. The best organization for them is private enterprise. If they employ a dozen people, the danger that the employer may exploit the workers can be perfectly well looked after by the unions. This is a very clear-cut matter; where the person who is responsible for the assets is identified, there is a real existential relationship between man and matter, material. Where countries have tried to socialize or nationalize those small businesses, the result was that you just couldn't get the work done any more. Also, the urge of many straightforward, honest people to stand on their own feet and do their own thing is frustrated: everybody has to become some sort of servant of a monster organization, a bureaucracy, to do anything. This makes a very poor life. So I have no doubt in my mind that at this level private enterprise is excellent.

You go to the other extreme if you have a huge factory, a huge company, whose every movement has a vast social and political impact. Then I think private ownership is just a pretense; it has no existential reality. The "owner" has no relationship to these assets. It's much like the pre-revolutionary French landowners who were living in Paris and just drew an unearned income from the workers or from the peasants. So there one has to look for arrangements to remove this pretense. But to think only in terms of state ownership gets one into endless trouble. My own conclusion is that government and business do not properly mix, and they must be kept separate. But that doesn't mean that one can't bring the social interest in. In Britain there is a tradition of the public corporation, and the division of powers has been fairly well worked out. When the coal mines were nationalized, or the electricity industry, or the gas industry, or the railroads, they were organized as public corporations: just as much companies as Imperial Chemical Industries or General Electric. There are many precise constitutional problems, because for everything there has to be an authority of last resort. In the Scott Bader Company, it's a board of trustees. If you have a democracy, it's easy to get rid of a government, but somebody has to see to it that the new government is formed.

When it's easy to get rid of the top man, then somebody has to see that there is a succession. In Britain

that is the function of the Queen; in the case of
Germany, it's the function of the President, and so on.
Equally with a nationalized industry: who is responsible
for there being a top-level board of management?
Sorry, I can't get away from hierarchies! In Britain it's a
minister; for the fuel industry it's the Minister of
Energy. He appoints the board, each person, separately.
This is a big mistake. I don't mind if the minister
appoints the chairman of the board; but then the
chairman must be allowed to assemble his team. If the
minister separately appoints the chairman, deputy
chairmen, board members, that's not the way to build a
team. And everything depends on teamwork. This is a
flaw in the arrangement. There can be rules, provisions
about the size of the board, and all that. Apart from this
flaw, on the whole the arrangement is very sensible. The
minister can appoint only the board; anything underneath the board, which are the chief executives on a vast
thing like the British Coal Board—we had a payroll of
850,000 people at the start—is appointed by the board. I
have never been on the board; I have been at the next
level. I even could make a public speech against nuclear
energy in 1967, which caused a fantastic furor and went
up to the Prime Minister. But the government couldn't
sack me; and since the board didn't sack me, I was
protected. It's vital to have protection against this "spoils
system," that anybody further down can be appointed
by government.

The management problem, when the company is big,
is absurdly great. Administration is really a very, very
difficult job. In the coal industry in Britain we all wished

we were mining engineers: that's an easy job, where you have to grapple with dead matter. But to grapple with living matter, that's much more difficult. You sit in an office and you have somehow to frame rules that fit reality. But reality is always even stranger than fiction. The style of management in a hierarchy should be the best possible style of management. If people don't consult, then it is just a bad style of management. At the Coal Board we always had excellent consultation, quite a way down, and all that. Well, administration is unbelievably difficult. It is really doing abstract justice to the concrete reality. If you now get your best brains up into the head office for administration, you are missing them down below, at the scene of action. It will be well administered, but the actual operations are done without first-class talent. And, if you get the first-class talent not at the top but down below, then it means you have second- and third-class talent administering, and the people down below are frustrated because of that so-and-so bureaucracy framing these stupid rules.

This has led me to the conviction that the best administration adheres to what I call the "negative theory of administration": Strive to find structures which need *minimum* administration. Very small structures administer themselves; there is no problem. It's not a matter of abstractly framing rules, because the human mind encompasses the whole thing and can make decisions *ad hoc,* and consultation of course is very easy.

When, however, you are landed with a big thing, what do you do? I had two pictures in my mind: one the picture of a Christmas tree, with a star at the top and all sorts of nuts underneath, more or less nourishing and useful nuts. That is a monolithic organization. The administrators, as particularly epitomized by accountants, always tend to such an orderly setup. The biggest task in any living thing is initiative. But, with this monolithic structure, one normally looks to the star at the top for the initiative because all the rest are executors of the policy. One man's initiative, no matter how able, and then a diminishing scale downwards of initiative is just not good enough to keep the thing alive.

Take the other picture—a chap at a fun fair, who in one hand holds hundreds of strings, and at the end of each string a balloon. Each balloon has its own buoyancy, a nice round thing. That is the ideal structure in a large organization. Of course you need someone to hold it all together, but it is not a star at the top, it is a man underneath and each balloon has its own buoyancy. Each balloon is somehow a limited thing, and thus, in a manner of speaking, the more the merrier.

So with this idea we thought, How can we reorganize or structurize this monolith? Simply to decentralize it and break it up was not an option, for quite insuperable reasons. First you want to reduce the total mass, and find out what are activities that *could* be separated out without paralyzing things. There are many activities that might just as well be done by outside firms. For example, the Coal Board had its own printing shops; well, printing and coal getting have very little in common. So let's take those activities out and organize them under a separate executive, which still is part of the whole thing but has its own identity.

In the historical process the first thing to be separated out was open-cast mining, what you call strip mining, which is something quite different from deep mining. This was taken out because the chap in charge of an area that does deep mining is not terribly interested in open-cast mining, nor does he have the expertise. That was the first executive, the open-cast executive.

Then, after the coal has come up the shaft, sometimes it is sold as it is, to power stations and so on, and sometimes it is processed, through coke ovens or other plants. And we found that this too is something quite different, which requires expert management and special expertise and all that, and which lends itself to being pulled out of the big mass. So we got the coal-products executive. And a few other things: we were landed with a lot of brickworks attached to the coal mines. The mine manager is not necessarily a very able brickworks manager, so that became the brickworks executive.

Then there are other activities, such as motor transport. The Coal Board was one of the biggest motor-transport undertakings. It takes certain management skills to do this well: buying, maintenance, repairing. It wants to be organized if you have between five and ten thousand enormous lorries, not only to cart the coal around but also to dump the shale, dispose of it. . . . Then the interesting things begin to appear, because you think, Well, all vehicles are to be put under a separate transport executive. Ah! Does that really make sense? Should that include the fire-fighting engines? Should that include the ambulances? You have to make distinctions. I insist that all this is hard work; there are no set formulas.

We are then left with a big mass of coal-getting proper. We divided this into seventeen areas, and then started sorting out which functions can be absolutely at the discretion of the area director. There the principle of "subsidiarity" comes in; that is, at headquarters we do not want to do anything that in fact they can do themselves. Only when they need help do we arrogate to ourselves this particular function. The functions that could not be decentralized or delegated downward were, for instance, negotiations with the union, overall financial arrangements, and certain parts of marketing policy.

Of course, a change in the system doesn't solve the problem. Gandhi once said scathingly, Everybody is looking for a system so perfect that no one inside has to be good. Such a system doesn't exist. Any organization has people in it, and the people are much the same people as are outside. All the same, if one changes the basis of ownership, it does open a door through which one can walk and do things that otherwise would be done in a sort of benevolent, patriotic spirit. And then it becomes the challenge, the natural thing to do. While a private firm can have a very good tone of management, with plenty of consultation, once you've changed the ownership pattern, then this becomes a constitutional duty. It's not left to the free will of the owner: you've got to do it, sometimes even if it doesn't immediately pay to do so. And the whole thing assumes that, perhaps idealizing it a little bit, the quality of people is there—a function which business does not normally fulfill. After all, people spend most of their energy on the job. Business is not there simply to produce goods, it also produces *people,* so that the whole thing becomes a learning process.

Rash nationalization, without being very, very carefully thought through, is almost invariably a disaster. Like any deep disturbance of a living thing, the very abruptness of change causes so much turmoil that it takes years to get straight again, and then finally to make use of the opportunity, to make it a change in the right direction.

There were three main activities which accrued to me at the same time that I had a full-time job as chief economist of the British Coal Board. All three are spare-time activities. (In Britain it's so difficult to raise money that anyone who says, First the money, and then we'll try to do something with the money, has very little chance of succeeding. I believe the best things have grown from people who said, Of course, I make my living, but there's plenty of time to do something else as well. The main thing is not to have to sponge off society.) These three activities are, first of all, the Soil Association, which is a private British organization to try to develop organic farming. We've been at it for the last thirty years. Of course, we have been ridiculed; but the wind is blowing in this direction, and we don't really know how to cope with it. We are overrun with people who want now to farm organically, but of course for

generations no farm manager had been trained. . . .
We get land offered, but we have to go through the
motions of training people first. We have infiltrated a
number of academic institutions and are running the
training with established institutions, which of course is
much easier than to build something up entirely *de novo*.

I am not impressed by the big power structures. As
power structures they are of course dangerous. But they
do happen to be run by *people*, individuals. The time has
come to work with the dinosaurs, the large corporations.

My son always takes initiatives. He wrote a letter the
other day to the British chairman of General Electric,
Sir Arnold Weinstock. No doubt he picked up something at home, but it was his letter. He wrote,

Dear Sir Arnold Weinstock:
  In view of the fuel crisis, which will not go away, and
in view of inflation, which also will not go away, and in
view of so many old and lonely people, why don't you
produce an electric mini-teakettle? It seems silly that
these old and lonely people should heat up two or three
pints of water just to make one cup of tea. If you would
do that, you would: (a) help to solve the fuel crisis; (b)
help to fight inflation; (c) help these old and lonely
people; (d) give us a good idea of what to give them for
Christmas or birthday; and (e) make a packet yourself.
If you would take up this idea, you might consider
sending me enough money to buy a bicycle, also to save
fuel; and, once you have produced it, a mini-teakettle
for my old dad.

He signed himself "Robert Schumacher, age 11."
  Well, the dinosaur replied within two days, on exquis-

ite notepaper, typed by the most wonderful electric typewriter:

Dear Mr. Schumacher:
  General Electric actually do not make small stuff, only very big stuff. But I must thank you for your most interesting letter. If you carry on with that amount of initiative, you will soon earn enough money to buy yourself a bicycle and also to support your old dad.
  Yours sincerely,
Arnold Weinstock.

Well, forgive me: this just came up. It is a memory. You see how one must deal with dinosaurs.

So the first organization I am involved with is the Soil Association. Our task currently is threefold. First of all, to organize the training for organic farmers. Second, we have set up a marketing company to market organic produce. In order to do this we had to invent an emblem, a trademark, so to speak, which we have registered with the authorities, who will not register a trademark saying, "This is organic produce," unless we are able to assure them that we can *monitor* it. It has been a lot of work to find out a method of monitoring. You can't monitor everything that comes off the farms, but you can monitor the soil. A German fellow has developed a very ingenious soil test, which we got accepted. That's a feasible proposition.

That's the marketing company, which can get the premium that organic produce deserves, because the value per ton or hundredweight of organic produce, even in scientific terms, is higher. The third thing is, we have now organized an organic farmers' cooperative. So that they can maintain their full independence They don't pool their farms, but it is a service cooperative, so that they can do some joint buying and other joint services. Now these things are going ahead, and the cooperative is helping the farmers to bring back into their hands more of the value added. For instance, if you have organically grown wheat, and you're not too far away from a market, why sell the wheat? Why not sell freshly ground flour? For this we have been able to find excellent small-scale milling equipment, and per pound of flour the farmers get twice the revenue they got per pound of wheat. So that value added is brought back into the farm economy, rather than being skimmed off by the miller. And of course the flour *is* better, freshly ground is better, organically grown is better, and it commands a better price: the value is higher.

The second link of my little chain is this company called Scott Bader, a plastics company founded by Ernest Bader, a Swiss Quaker immigrant to England before the First World War. He's now about eighty-five. Ernest Bader was penniless when he started in England. He said, All my life I will have to work for others. What a dreadful system. Well, it didn't work out like that. He was an entrepreneur and he had a business and in 1951 he suddenly woke up and said, I am now doing to all these people what I suffered from when it was done to me. I am not going to go out of this life with this feeling. No, I must do something. So he got in touch with various people, including myself, and said, I want to put

this on a basis that I as a Quaker and a pacifist believe in.
I don't believe in what I am doing. And so we worked
very hard and hammered out a constitution for this
firm. Ernest Bader said, No, I don't want to have
ownership of this company, and so all the capital, except
10 percent, was vested in the commonwealth, which was
set up for this purpose as a limited company. The equity
doesn't lie anymore with Ernest Bader, it lies with that
commonwealth, and everybody who works for a certain
length of time becomes a member of the commonwealth. Legally speaking, the commonwealth is the
owner of the operating company. At first the family
retained 10 percent founder's share, so arranged that
they had a majority, not with the intention of using it
but as a last resort. Because it is jolly difficult to build
something up but it is very easy to ruin it.

We then tried to learn the business. What does
participation mean? Can you run the thing so that you
actually give people the "absolute" security that if trade
is bad we won't suddenly draw a line and say to you,
"Out," in order to protect our livelihood? No, this is a
livelihood, this is a community, a solidarity. How can it
be done? That is the question. Everybody told us it
couldn't be done. What do you do if suddenly trade
slumps, and your competitors lay off 50 percent of their
work force and you have to carry the whole thing? Well,
there's no use reading books about these things; one has
to feel them on one's own skin. It leads to quite a
different kind of management. The demands on management are greater.

We have to think ten times before we expand at the

start, because we know once they are with us we belong together. In this sense there are no owners and employees; we are all co-owners and co-employees. It was not until 1963, that is, twelve years later, that we felt it worked. The founder's shares were also put into the general pocket of the commonwealth, so it is the administration of the commonwealth that owns the thing. In fact you might say ownership has been abolished. It has not been transferred to any individuals. Because a member of the commonwealth, when he wants to leave, move to another part of the country, or doesn't like it anymore, does not take with him a slice of Scott Bader. Instead of all the rights of ownership and all those different rights simply being with the owner, we now have to ask, What happens with the money? What happens with the management? In free personal capitalism everything is automatically "mine," it all rests with me as the owner and this makes a lot of sense if I am a working owner. But we now have to think it out and distribute it and we learn a great deal. Participation, of course, is a hallowed word and we all approve of it, and say, Well, you know, democratization. . . . What precisely does it mean? People say, Well, we don't want a hierarchical structure. Well, can you run the thing without some hierarchy?

These questions have now been practiced in reality in the Scott Bader case for twenty-seven years. And one can only use the famous phrase "I have seen the future and it works." The company has gone from strength to strength.

We imposed upon ourselves a number of what I call

"self-denying ordinances." One of them is, Being of Quaker origin, we will not knowingly sell any of our products if we have reason to believe it will be used for armaments.

The second one is that a sort of parliament of workers is the sovereign body, not the board of directors. And they can, in fact, choose or dismiss directors, and have to approve the salaries of chairman and directors. In that respect, there's a high degree of democracy. Also, there are constitutional provisions for real participation in decision making.

Another one is that we have settled the maximum spread between the highest paid and the lowest paid: that is, before tax. It may shock many people that, in spite of a lot of good will from all concerned, that spread is still one to seven. There is no pressure from the community that it should be narrowed, because it is understood that this spread is necessary. But of course this includes everybody, the lowest-paid juvenile compared with the highest-paid senior employee.

The fourth self-denying ordinance is that we are determined not to grow beyond the size of four hundred. Now, you can ask, Four hundred? Why not three hundred and fifty? Just as in nature a cell doesn't expand and expand, but when there is a requirement of growth it splits and makes a new cell, so we have, under great pressures of growth, split and have put into being three new companies, totally independent. That requires a bit of brainwork, to determine where you can separate it off. But the primary concern is to keep the human touch.

The final ordinance is that when there are profits—and there have always been profits—some money must be put aside for taxation and reinvestment. A maximum of 40 percent is available for distribution. But for every pound that we distribute to ourselves, we set one pound aside for some external noble purpose. So up to 40 percent of the profits can be distributed, half to our members and half for some good purpose outside.

The idea was that with this money we wanted to get involved with the requirements of the neighborhood. But within fifty miles, we couldn't find anything that needed doing. I mean in this little firm, only four hundred people, over the course of almost thirty years, everything that other regions are crying out for has been looked after. The old people are looked after: they get their regular parcels. The boys' club wanted a baseball diamond: they've got it. The association of the blind wanted help with their Braille: they've got it. The embarrassment now is that we can't find any new purpose in the neighborhood. This is very important: if the wealth is really utilized in the neighborhood it comes from, then actually all problems can be solved. The social problems anyway. So we have to go further afield, but just to hand it over to some national charity is witless: we don't want to do that. It's a big job.

Scott Bader is more than an experiment, it's a lifestyle. Yet, in our primary purpose, which had been the humanization of the work process, in all these years we've not made much headway. We are hooked there on a technology—as the English schoolchild says of the chemistry lesson, he says it "stinks," and a chemical factory stinks. And it is a process that cannot be humanized. We might one day say, Well, then, we won't make polyester; we will do something quite different. . . . But meantime, we thought, we can't humanize the thirty-eight hours a week that people work for their living, but what about the other more than a hundred hours a week that they're anyhow not in the laboratory, not in the office, not in the factory? There we found very quickly that infinite boredom prevails, which leads people to look at television. And that doesn't make anybody happy.

We said, Surely the community can develop activities, useful activities, for utilizing their spare time. And there again, we started by suggesting, Why don't you build yourselves a community motorcar repair shop? You're all clever chaps with your hands and brains. Those who have a motorbike can be seen every weekend sitting surrounded by the parts of the motorbike, enjoying themselves hugely by pulling it to pieces and putting it together again. But with a car you can't do it, because the thing is too heavy: you don't have the gear. They then built themselves a community motorcar repair shop. We got two old-age pensioners to look after it; they're happy, they've got something to do, thank God. And when a car breaks down, they take the car to their own garage and repair it, and the cost is just the cost of materials. That is an extension of the whole idea of community.

The next thing is, every Englishman has a little garden, so we had a simple idea: really good gardening tools and machines. Little chaps, they buy a thing and find it doesn't really work; it's a flimsy job. So we got very good people to advise us, and· created a gardening-machine pool, again run by a number of old-age pensioners, and everybody has access to really superlative tools and they've all become passionately interested in growing things, not just keeping their lawns shorn.

The next step has not yet been implemented. We have actually some land, but Ernest Bader—most unreasonably!—doesn't want this land to be used for vegetable production. He says, I live here, and this has been my parkland. The committee says, We are dying to grow vegetables, but we are not going to offend the old man. I mention this rather touching incident because it shows that the relationship between the worker and the boss, the accursed capitalist and the exploited workers, has entirely ceased. We would not do a thing which we all know is reasonable. We know the old chap is unreasonable in his high old age, but we would not offend him. We would rather wait. Now *that's* reasonable!

The next thing that is now in the planning stage is a commonwealth woodworking shop, because they say, We can make our own furniture; we can even go further and make a surplus of furniture for local sale. So we shall see. But on the basis of this little firm having been put on a common ownership basis, which of course seemed a most generous act on the part of the owner, a new life-style is gradually developing, which may in fact take off the pressure on the need to earn wages, so that we could reduce the working hours, and perhaps we can leave it free to people to choose. But whether it is forty hours a week, or thirty-eight, it is still a full-time job, and if it's mindless work it has a very bad effect on the worker. I think if it were twenty hours it would be just a chore, for a few hours every day, and human nature can stand that.

The third organization I'm concerned with is one that I started with a handful of friends in 1965: the Intermediate Technology Development Group, Limited. In the U.S. you would call it "incorporated," but "limited" is a better word—it's more descriptive.

Now you have the company, charity status, no money, maybe somebody has let you share an office, but what actually do you want to do? You want to create and systematize this intermediate technology, but how do you set about doing this? All I can say at this early stage is, Beware of the planners. There are all sorts of impatient people who will say, You must have a five-year plan, a ten-year plan. Quite useless. You must realize your nonknowledge, what you don't know. The inner attitude if you think you know is quite different from the attitude when you know you don't know. You're much more observant, more alert.

And it happened that we heard that a British trade mission was going to Nigeria, and we thought, My goodness, what are they going to flog in Nigeria? Certainly not the stuff the Nigerians really need. What if we made, very rapidly, a catalog of hand- and animal-propelled agricultural equipment obtainable in Britain? We had only a few weeks to do it, and under this pressure we found that our society is very highly organized. You have only to find out how to touch the network; the network already exists. There is an association of agricultural engineers, one of producers of agricultural equipment. We got in touch with all of them and produced a little catalog, stenciled, of animal- and man-operated agricultural equipment obtainable from little hole-and-corner firms in Britain.

When the mission went to Nigeria, they were most astonished. This thing was torn out of their hands by people who said, For the first time you bring us something that is of interest, instead of the usual glossy catalogs; and that gave us a clue as to what needed doing. We said, Of course this is a rough job; let's do a bigger job, not limited to agricultural equipment. And in 1967 we produced a big catalog, called *Tools for Progress: a Guide to Small Scale Equipment for Rural Development.* In 1967, after twenty years of aid, so called, which had involved many billions of dollars, this was the first time that somebody made a catalog of suitable equipment for developing countries, and it caused a sensation. Although we were operating out of one small room, and had no sales apparatus, this catalog rolled around the globe, It actually became a commercially profitable proposition; we borrowed money for it and we paid it off again.

In this catalog the manufacturer had to pay for having his product included; some things got in that we didn't want in, and some were left out. Also it was limited to Britain because we had no money to travel. So it was a superficial job and we found we had to dig deeper. We came to the decision that this had to be done systematically subject by subject as opportunity served.

Now, if you want to do something effective, the first decision you have to make is, are you going to work in your own back yard, turning your back on big, rich society, or are you going to harness the society to do the work for you? We decided that the needs were far too urgent to go the comfortable way of puttering around in our own back yards; we must find the ways and means of roping in the big society. How do you do it? Well, there is a lot in the organization structure that needs to be observed. Let's have a structure like nature with little cells. To each cell we can attach people. If we have just one cell that grows bigger and bigger it's not flexible enough. And so we took up one subject after another and set up specialized panels: building, agricultural equipment, water, power, rural health cooperatives, etc. The first one was building. Let's organize this as if it were a separate little company and let's invite people from outside, on a voluntary basis, to give us their advice. We have plenty of people interested in this. Often they just approach us and say they want to do this kind of work. That's the way it happens.

The building panel was twelve people who had been invited to help us on the question of the poor man's building problem. Why in Africa do they have to have South African or European or American contractors to do the bigger jobs? What sort of people do we want on this building panel? There are three main forces in society, we call them A, B, and C. A are government people, administrators. We want them with us. How can we find in all this some sympathetic character who would like to join in the work? That's the A factor. But

85

let's face it, government can't do anything, really. They can stop things, finance things, they know the ropes; but government is not a daring center of initiative and creativity. So we need a B factor. B is business; after all, business is what does the work. And in business lies the knowhow and also lies the discipline of viability, how to make things so that you can pay your wages on Friday. We must have that particular element on our side. And C are the communicators, the people of the word. They don't actually produce anything like lettuce or bread, but they produce ideas and generally speaking (and I mean this in a very kindly way) they are very playful souls. They fall in love with the problem, they solve the problem, mark it top secret, and file it away, fall in love with the next problem. . . .   It is of course a resource, but only a resource. If somebody has the organizing power to make these ideas work and put them into flesh, that's ABC. Now of course if the C factor has done some productive work, wants to file it away, then the B factor will say, We spent some money on it, we now must get it applied, push it out. The C factor doesn't want to do that; it would be soiling his hand by becoming commercial. Well, one has to make up one's mind. If one wants to maintain a sort of noncommercial virginity one cannot become really fertile. So each of the panels is composed of these three forces. When they come together they discover that the other two, of whom they have had a very low opinion, are quite good people, and they enjoy it. This is very effective.

To have voluntary people who come together to give sage advice is wonderful, but how is the work going to be done? We want to know, from the best information we can get, what needs doing. Among the building panel the thing was very interesting. I have always had very simple, stupid ideas. I have, perhaps, a bit of a gift to reduce things to their basic simplicity, and I ask questions like, What is a building anyhow? I come up with the answer: four posts with a roof. The posts are not the problem, the roof is. So I thought the building panel would advise us that we should make a proper study of roof construction, roof materials, suitable in poor countries, and the like. But they said something quite different. They said, No, the missing factor in the building field is not material, it is that architects, civil engineers, bricklayers, plumbers, etc., get trained, but the one man who is supposed to take the contract and hold the thing together has been forgotten. Even if you work out a new technology, there is no one to receive it except these architects, etc. You must begin at the beginning and that is the contractor.

Our purpose is not to get a lot of dogs and then do our own barking, and so when we got this advice we asked, What can we do about it? Well, you have to train the contractors. Is this acceptable? Do they want to be trained? Well, let's discover what the situation is in Nigeria. Lo and behold we quickly find that actually the Nigerian contractors turned out to be extremely teachable, delightful people and several years' work was done to produce the teaching materials thoroughly tested for indigenous contractors. From Nigeria this thing has leaped to East Africa and elsewhere. We feel as far as that is concerned we have filled a knowledge gap but we don't want to become a specialized institution training contractors. No, now everybody can do it. This knowledge gap has been filled.

The building panel says, *Now* we can turn to building materials, particularly roofing. There my intuition was quite correct; they confirmed it. But how do you build a roof when you have no steel and no timber? How did our forefathers do it? They very often did it with vaulting. Now what is the applicability of that? What methods, etc.? There is bamboo in many places. Can this be used with real modern intelligence but still keeping it so simple that the little villager can build a really good roof? While traveling around the world, I've always asked the building authorities what materials they needed and they said corrugated iron, in another place aluminum, and in the next place it's something different. Nobody has done the work. It's all hit and miss. Our building panel is now working on roof-construction materials and methods and will soon come up with very interesting results showing that there are quite astonishing things that can be done with very simple materials.

This is ITDG's structure. But for a panel to be able to work we then attach to the panel a permanent officer who has to be paid. We don't always succeed. Each thing is organized as a separate project and has to be separately funded, and we don't always succeed in getting the funding and then we can't have a permanent chap, but we try to keep it going in some way. Normally our permanent staff member has the task of finding some agency where the work can be done. For instance, the agricultural-equipment panel says we must survey the whole world for really useful agricultural equipment, make sure it is verified, look at operating conditions, and then publish it, not with a vague description but with line drawings so that the village blacksmith, perhaps with a bit of help, can make it on the spot. Where do you do this work? It's not a work that you do in industry; it's a work that's done at some academic institution. So we infiltrated ourselves into the National College of Agricultural Engineering, which is situated in Bedfordshire. From there we created an international unit—of course they have land, students, professors— and we got prototypes of various equipment. We studied, and when we were thoroughly satisfied our booklet was published. This is now a series of publications which go into all countries, simple, down to earth, proven agricultural equipment.

The work of our unit encouraged the staff and students at the National College to start thinking the same way. One of the machines they developed is a "walking mini-tractor." It isn't terribly clever to send two tons of extremely expensive machinery called a tractor backward and forward over the field, compacting the soil and making life very troublesome for the soil bacteria; they can't breathe properly. And all this for the sake of pulling a curved knife, a plow. Wouldn't it be easier and better if we could just pull the plow without having to pull the whole weight of the tractor.

Now, a young engineer at the college—his name is Barney Muckle—recalled that our forefathers used semi-stationary engines in this way; but they never completed the method, and they didn't have the engines that we have today. So a team set to work to improve on the old method, and they came up with a machine they christened the Snail. It's not for fast plowing on a two-thousand-acre farm in the U.S. but that's not the problem in the developing countries. The problem is that the farms are three, five, seven acres, for which the tractor is a nuisance anyhow. This Snail has a fuel cost per acre which is 1/100 of tractor plowing. In fact, you can forget about fuel costs. It also has a capital cost of 1/100 of tractor cost. It really is a technology for the poor who *ipso facto* operate on a small scale. Again, I'm not saying it's the right thing everywhere, but it certainly increases the choice, because the little engine looks like a sewing machine. You can take it under your arm and walk away with it. Maybe in certain applications this is not the answer, but bullocks. This has to be weighed on the spot by the operators. The joy of reality is that the Snail doesn't have to be stabled, fed, except with a bit of oil, but of course it doesn't produce any muck. The bullock does. You have to weigh one against the other. You can't do that at a desk; you have to do it as a practical farmer. But now at least he has an engine that is so cheap he can afford it and fuel consumption is a minimum.

We have so many publications now that we have pulled all that out of the main organization and set up a separate company. Intermediate Technology Publications, Ltd., which is wholly owned by the charitable organization, but works with commercial discipline.

In Burma, before I was there, there was a British military station, about twenty or thirty miles away from a town, and in order to get the mail to the people the British authorities hired an Indian chap with a horse and a coach to bring the mail. They were prepared to pay him—not his entire costs because the coach was fitted to take passengers and the road from this military station to the town was a very busy road, lots and lots of people walking or oxcarts very slowly moving along. This Indian carried the mail back and forth for a year, and when the year was out he came back and said, I can't go on doing it at that price. Why not? Because I can't get any passengers. Why can't you get passengers? The coach is convenient, plenty of people, the price is perfectly reasonable and they all have money. Well then, finally someone—he had probably been to Harvard business school—said, Let's ask the consumer. They asked the consumers, these people who are walking twenty miles in the hot sun, Why don't you use the coach, it only costs a couple of rupees? They said, Look at the horses, the horses shouldn't be pulling a coach; they should be out on the grass. We would never demean ourselves to travel behind horses that are so ill kept. We'd rather walk.

Before we can publish we must be quite sure that the thing works. Not only works under the conditions of poor countries, but also it must have social acceptability. We are quite pleased about one development which our agricultural panel induced. So much mechanization of agriculture has been a total failure and we wondered why. Basically, simplifying it, it is because here we have someone who has an absolutely marvelous weeding machine or implement. So he says, That's what they need. Out he goes, he shows them this technical marvel, and they, of course, equally as enchantable by technology as we are, they say yes. Then you come again a year later and it's rusting somewhere. It is totally useless for them. So we want to make sure that the equipment is wanted. It is wanted when, with their current methods, they can't do the job properly because the workload is too great.

It is necessary to measure the workload through the first months of the work year. And you find the characteristic curve which has a peak when everyone is out in the fields and then it has troughs where everybody is sitting around with nothing to do. You may have several peaks. And then you say, Well, here at the peak they are overextended, and unless I break through I am not helping them. That's where we need some mechanical help. Down here, it may be a laborious chore, but so few people are involved, if I now bring in capital goods to reduce the labor, I merely increase the items and reduce the cash resources in the village. I am not doing them any good whatsoever. All this has been reduced to a very simple method so that we don't need studied people to do the assessment; we get school leavers to do it. We will not talk about mechanization of agriculture in general but only for specific localities after this ascertainment has taken place. Then you don't have any problem of the peasants accepting it because they know perfectly well what is right and what is wrong. If they are not seduced by aid, if they have to pay for it themselves, they are very shrewd. And of course they have to pay for all the things themselves because we have no money.

Many of the technologies that we have so far developed are meant to be capital saving. They are capital saving, so they are in reach of the poor, but many of them are too labor intensive; they are too much work. We always look for improvements. We never talk about this labor-intensive technology as being desirable, because slogging away is nothing particularly desirable.

In order to have intimate contact with industry we have a unit called Intermediate Technology Industrial Services. This is now financed by the Ministry of Overseas Development. They find that they can't act effectively unless they work intimately with industry, but for government to work with industry is extremely difficult because there are rules. The industrialists think, Oh, here is the big purse, now maybe we can get big money there. It's very difficult for government. So government works with us, the industrialist works in his own unit, and we work with industry. We are, as it were, the differential between those two wheels which go at different speeds.

Two more points. We want to help the poor but in the poor countries not everybody is poor. Some poor countries have far more money than is good for them, like the OPEC countries. Why should we do charitable work for the OPEC countries? If they want me to go there, I take off my charitable hat and put on my commercial hat of another company, which is Intermediate Technology Services, Ltd., a purely commercial company, and I recycle the petrodollars. This helps to finance the charitable work we are doing.

The final problem is to reach the people for whom we

are working in the third world. How do you reach two million villagers? There is no ready answer. We try to persuade the developing countries to set up a counterpart organization in their own country. Let's take Sri Lanka, the last country I visited a few months ago. If you have such an intermediate technology organization in Colombo you have a better chance of getting in touch with the little people in Sri Lanka than if you have it in London. Ideally I would want to deal only with these counterpart groups around the world and create a network. Quite a number of these groups have been set up. They're not ours; they're theirs. They are purely indigenous. Some are more successful than others. I think the most successful ones, which go quite a few years back, are in Ghana and India. They are really standing on their own two feet, and if anybody wants our help in Ghana or India we can immediately say, Well, first go to the Technology Consulting Centre at Kumasi in Ghana, or the Appropriate Technology Development Association in Lucknow, India. And if they need help from us they will find a way. It must become a network, otherwise it is unmanageable.

This applies also to the rich counries. Actually, and not so surprisingly, the rich countries are now waking up to their own problems, namely, that the rural areas are being drained of people, that there has to be a redevelopment that we thought hitherto was necessary only for the third world. So in a number of them intermediate technology groups for local use have come into being.

To summarize, ITDG's activities are based on five convictions:

The source and center of world poverty lies primarily in the rural areas of poor countries, which tend to be bypassed by aid and development as currently practiced.

The rural areas will continue to be bypassed and unemployment as well as the drift of migration into cities will continue to grow unless efficient, small-scale technologies are made available with assistance in their use.

The donor countries and agencies do not at present possess the necessary organized knowledge of adapted, appropriate technologies and communications to be able to assist effectively in rural development on the scale required.

In matters of development there is a problem of choosing the right "level of technology" to fit the given circumstances; in other words, there is a *choice* of technology and it cannot be assumed that the level of technology used by affluent societies is the only possible level, let alone that it is necessarily the best for poor societies.

The technologies most likely to be appropriate for development in conditions of poverty would be in a sense "intermediate" between—to speak symbolically—the hoe and the tractor, or the panga and the combine harvester.

Knowhow at this intermediate level, and the relevant equipment, obviously existed in many places, but no one could say what *gaps* there were, and there was no point anywhere in the world where this knowhow could be obtained as and when the people most in need of it required it. Intermediate Technology *Development* means the work of bringing this kind of knowledge to light, systematizing and, where necessary, completing it, and organizing a world-wide system of "knowledge centers" where it can be readily found.

Ten years of work in this field have supplied the Group with plentiful evidence that the "knowledge gap" it set out to fill is indeed very wide. Technologies applicable on a small scale by or in communities with plenty of labor and little capital, lacking technical and organizational sophistication, are on the whole poorly documented, difficult to get hold of, and in many cases even nonexistent. There are numerous instances where the relevant knowledge and equipment used to exist but have virtually disappeared, in accordance with the well-known tendency of the "better" to be the enemy of the "good." This tendency is of course progressive and therefore to be welcomed, unless it deprives large numbers of people who cannot afford the "better" of the "good" they could afford.

4. On Appropriate Forms of Ownership and Action

The party's over and we have now to see what happens after the party. I'm not saying this is the end of the world, but certain structures, certain ways of life, have been created during these last roughly hundred years based on cheap and plentiful fossil fuels and based on a few other things. What other things? I will say, We had this party. Some of us enjoyed it. We were entertained by three great magicians, illusionists. One was the illusion that somehow, against all laws of nature, infinite growth in a finite environment is possible. That illusion of course has been attacked by many people for quite a long time. But it was then exploded by *The Limits to Growth* report. Now mankind listens because one could say that the computer has spoken, not just the human voice.

The second entertainer said that by some strange law of nature there is an unlimited supply of people who are prepared to do mindless repetitive work for quite modest remuneration. The same sort of illusion that was fostered in slave-owning societies about the slaves. Now people are waking up and discovering their power, discovering that without them the party would never have happened, that they are actually needed—much more than I. And this means a fundamental shift in power, which is not the same in every country. Some countries are ahead in this development and some are lagging behind. We have to rethink the whole industrial system.

The third illusion, which is still rampant, is that science can solve all problems. I have no doubt that science can solve any individual problem when it's clearly defined. But my experience is that as it solves problem A it creates a whole host of new problems. It's quite a thought that there are more scientists alive today than there have been in all previous human history taken together. What do they all do? They solve problems very efficiently. Aren't we running out of problems? No. We have more and more. This seems to be a bottomless pit. They grow faster than we solve them. So this is where we have to ask, What on earth is going on here? At the height of success, with technological competence unequaled in all human history, we read nothing but questions of survival. What did our forefathers do? They survived, obviously, without all these scientists. And without all these problems. So we have to ask ourselves if something has gone wrong in the development of technology, that finest thing we've got for our material life. These entertainers turn out to be illusions, but we still talk to each other as if these entertainers would return. They won't. They can't. Because of plentiful fossil fuel and a plentiful supply of labor prepared to be pushed around and put on assembly belts and so on, we have created a particular technology.

This technology is very unkind to living nature all around us. Living nature can take many knocks, it is tolerant. It has tolerance margins. But the massive assaults, even if only in a few places, lead to great ecological problems. This technology is also very selective in terms of the raw materials it requires, particularly the fuels. We could quarrel about exactly when, but there is no doubt that either sooner or later, and I think rather sooner than later, we shall have to learn to utilize much less of the fossil fuels, capital fuels as I call them, and much more of the income fuels. But the income fuels come in very small parcels and cannot be used by massive overlarge technology, technology that depends on an enormous concentration of fuel. So all these different problems are very closely connected with this technological development, which was logical in its own way, but ceases now to be logical, and we have somehow to find a way out of this inheritance of the last hundred years.

What can we do? We should attend to the problems that we can attend to. I remember a conversation between an elderly lady and a young lady. The young lady said, I am about to be married. You've been married for a long time, how do you ever manage to agree with your husband? The older lady replied, It's really very easy, I deal with the unimportant things and he deals with the important things. And so the young lady said, Give me some examples. Well, how we spend our income, of course I deal with that, and which school the children are going to, and whether we should move and where we live. Then the young one said, What on earth does your husband deal with? Well, with the big problems: whether China should be a member of the United Nations and how to reform the government in Washington. This is the modus operandi, we are always in danger of becoming too clever about these things and not noticing what we in fact can do and the act of doing will keep us cheerful. It is quite amazing how much theory one can do without when one starts real work.

We must do what we conceive to be the right thing and not bother our heads or burden our souls with whether we're going to be successful. Because if we don't do the right thing, we'll be doing the wrong thing and we'll be just part of the disease and not a part of the cure. My only business, the only real job we have, is to look after, to the best of our ability, the little people who can't help themselves. If education and the advantages that we have had from society are only so that we might form a sort of trade union of the privileged, then our soul is so burdened with darkness that life is not worth living. The requirements of these little people who can't help themselves are very simple. They don't have to go to the stars; they just want to know where tomorrow's meal is coming from. They want to have housing, they want to have clothing, they want to have a little culture. And if, as a society, we turn over some of our resources to the study of these humble requirements, then I think the road is free.

You can't be alive today without being interested in China, because it's the biggest transformation that's happened in the twentieth century. This enormous country, sick unto death for so many decades, suddenly, in one generation, turns itself around. People are fed, cheerful, everybody's at work, enthusiastic, they're all drably but adequately clothed, children are in fantastically good shape, full of buoyancy and cheerfulness. If you compare that with China in the 1920s and 1930s, it's a miraculous transformation. It's still a very, very poor society. But it's a poor society where the basic requirements are being met.

Various things have happened. Virtually from the demise of the Manchus in 1911 until Mao in 1948–49 were years of the most intense suffering. Out of this suffering there were born some people, undoubtedly of quite extraordinary intellectual power and stature, such as Mao and Chou En-lai, and they have built a new society there. As an economist, I would say what they have done primarily is to turn economics the other way around. Our type of economics says, You mustn't do anything, mustn't produce anything, unless you are quite sure you couldn't possibly buy it cheaper from outside. When I was in Puerto Rico, a luscious island, I found that the carrots were imported from Texas! You mustn't produce carrots in Puerto Rico if the Texas-produced carrots are cheaper. That's our system. The Chinese have turned this around. They have said, You mustn't buy anything from outside unless you can be quite sure you can't make it yourself. It's as simple as that. When you say, You mustn't produce unless you are quite sure you couldn't buy it more cheaply, then development is impeded. On the other hand, when you say you mustn't buy it unless it is really impossible for you to make it, economically speaking everybody is challenged, everybody is busy.

Another very important idea that the Chinese have worked out is that it takes thirty peasant work-years to keep a young person at a university for one year. If a person has been at a university for five years, by the time he is finished he has consumed 150 peasant work-years. And so that old brute Mao said, Well, young person, what are the peasants going to get for this? After all, it's a big peasant society; you have been educated at the cost of the peasants. You have consumed 150 peasant work-years. Instead of going to a fashionable district in Shanghai, you will go to a remote village and give something back to the peasants out of what you have learned. They went there, and they found they had nothing to give them; all that they had learned was totally irrelevant. They couldn't even weigh babies without a baby scale that cost far more than the whole income of the village. They came back and said, We don't learn at universities anything that is of any use. (This has a magical effect on the curriculum.)

Then they came to the next step and said, We must work and study together. Walk on both feet: a typical Chinese concept. A little period of study, then a little period of work. No one is too precious to do actual work, physical work. We must expose everybody to the reality of things. If they don't work, they don't know anything about reality; they know only what's written in books. They have everywhere insisted that people should have a small-scale technology and experience.

This transformation of China has been based on the idea of learning by doing. Not in the narrow sort of extreme-left sense, that only the workers, *they* know, but in accordance with Mao's teaching, namely that the manager or the intellectual has to go and learn from the workers. He then has to take back into his study what he has learned, make a theory out of it, and go and teach the workers *That* is the proper process. If the process is only half of that, either learning only from the workers or learning only from the managers, the theory is likely to be worthless.

ITDG has been under increasing criticism that we devote all our humble efforts to the third world and the rest of the world says to us, "What about us? We need an intermediate technology—an efficient technology." One province of Canada said, "We hear that you are dealing with intermediate technology for rural areas, but look what's becoming of the province. We are a *colony* of Toronto. We have been reduced to monoculture: wheat, wheat, wheat, nothing but wheat. Life is becoming intolerably dull. The things that we used to make ourselves now come in cellophane packages from Toronto. All the young people are leaving," they said. "The average age of the rural population of Saskatchewan is sixty-six years. We are a dying society! We don't want to die. We don't want the young people to leave, and they don't want to leave and crowd together in Toronto. But there is nothing else but wheat. So your intermediate technology, couldn't it help us?"

It was lunchtime and they served me some bread. I looked at this surrogate bread (already sliced) and I said, "Where does this come from?" "Toronto." "And the wheat in the bread?" "Oh, maybe that comes from Saskatchewan." "And why, please, don't you make your bread in Saskatchewan?" "Oh, in this day and age, surely that would be entirely uneconomic!" The reply was obvious: "Make up your minds whether you want to die economically or survive uneconomically."

If they put only a small part of their intelligence in the direction of systematically developing a small-scale technology that would fit their area, then they could even live economically, instead of only dying uneconomically. But this is not always easy to sell to people, the majority of whom cannot imagine anything except what they have in front of their eyes. They say, Our whole life experience is just the opposite; now you come with this sort of crazy notion.

We had very interesting negotiations with the brick industry in Britain. A hundred years ago the brickworks would produce ten thousand bricks a week. Around fifty years ago, a hundred thousand, about ten years ago, a million. And now two or three million. What does this mean? It means enormous units, and either they are near the biggest markets or require enormous commitment to transport. With the increased cost of transport, of oil, of labor, it costs as much to ship a brick two hundred miles overland as to make it. Therefore, a big brickworks with a market scattered all over the country is economic nonsense. But this economic nonsense doesn't correct itself until somebody creates the efficient mini-brickworks. We are in a phase where nobody believes this is possible, and, therefore, bricks simply become more expensive. The situation doesn't correct itself. Our task is to persuade our friends in big industry to make these design studies, and we have got a long way in our work, primarily for the developing countries. At the same time our brick expert builds a very big brickworks in England near Bristol, where there is a very big market—and a mini-brickworks in Ghana.

People talk about paper recycling, but do they really think about it properly? Here is a huge paper mill or a huge printing office—let's say the *New York Times*—and the paper is scattered all over the country. Are you going to collect it all and bring it back to one point? That would be foolish. It can't possibly pay. It would be too demanding on transport. Once it's scattered, it can be recycled only on a small scale. Talking about this not so very long ago, I was approached afterward by a chap from the biggest paper producers in Britain. He was interested and asked if we were really working on this. Yes, I told him, we are desperately keen to get a mini paper-recycling plant. We know there are big ones; but the big ones fit only into the biggest conurbations, the biggest megalopolises. So he said, Well, of course, it can be done on a small scale. We've never thought about it. But we have a little research tool—a mini-plant. Why don't you come and see us? We went to see them, and to cut a long story short they said, You're right. This is the wave of the future. You can have all our research resources to perfect this plant. And the design studies have now been completed. It doesn't cost us any money because they have seen what is really coming.

Now then, one asks oneself, They're so generous; in

business one hand washes the other. What is their advantage in giving us all these facilities? If they're perfectly frank they say, The way we have grown up, the way we are constituted, we could deal with one five-million-pound plant in a certain stretch of time; but if it's a hundred little contracts that is not what we could cope with. So we are delighted that you are pioneering this because, when it's ready, then perhaps it will be our lifeboat.

I was invited to visit a very large farm in southern England. The owner had been a member of the Soil Association. He's been a member from the start in 1947, but his farm was run along entirely different lines—highly chemicalized and so on. He was a deeply worried man when he showed me how dependent he had become on the industrial system, and if anything really went wrong, then the farm would collapse. He was unhappy. And as we were going across the farm—it was so big we were driving across in a Land-Rover—he stopped the car and said, "Do you see that land over there? There's two hundred acres just coming up for sale. I think I'll buy them. It would nicely round off the property." And I asked, "How are you going to farm it?" "Well, the same way as the other two thousand acres." "Why do you do it? You're worried because you don't believe you have the right system. Why don't you use this as your lifeboat? Learn an alternative system. You can't learn it from books; you have to do it!" He said, "You're absolutely right! That's what we ought to do. But actually I am not the owner, this is owned by a company, and whether my fellow directors will agree I very much doubt." It took him six months, and I got a letter. He was very happy that his corps of directors now agreed. They are running a lifeboat farm, trying the opposite methods, the organic methods, not dependent on the big industrial system. And it turned out that his fellow directors were his son and his nephew. There was harmony in the family.

It's very interesting to learn where the support comes from and where the opposition comes from. Support comes normally from people in big business. Apparently they have been rubbing against reality all their lives so they can understand these things. But, strange to say, the intellectuals, who ought to be the most wide awake, get flustered. They get annoyed. They ask strange questions. They say, Well, even if you are right, once you have introduced intermediate technology, how can you make sure it doesn't become big technology once again? Questions that are, as it were, tangents going into empty space. Or they say, This is all very good, but *in fact,* you can't do anything because the system will not allow it. Or they try to involve me in discussions of whether I am in favor of growth or against growth. This attitude worries me. We need the open-mindedness and realism and toughness of those in big business—we need it to help us. But we also need the intellectuals, people of the word, communicators, research people, and of course those in governments.

The interest now is most lively in some of the advanced countries. For instance, in Britain, the biggest county is Yorkshire. And a number of Yorkshiremen said, Why don't you work with us for Yorkshire? I said,

Because we are working for the third world, and that is what we want to do. But you're quite right, why don't you set up an intermediate technology in Yorkshire? At first it sounded strange to them, but the Yorkshireman—who considers himself the backbone of Britain—said yes. Unemployment is rising. Budgetary allocations from central government are falling. Why don't we do it? Why don't we stand on our own little feet, and put our own chaps to work? Of course we can't put them to work the way big society has done hitherto, because they are unemployed. And a workplace with a capitalization of $50,000—we haven't got that kind of money from the big system. But we can develop and deploy an intermediate technology where you can become productive with very little capital. I can show you again and again that with very little capital you can get productivity that is higher than the chap's with a lot of capital. I'm not talking about moon shots; I'm not talking about aircraft; I'm talking about the basic things of human life—like building materials, cement.

Yes, cement. Can't we have a mini-plant for cement? What's the point of making it all in one place and then carting it all over the countryside? The developing countries, the rural areas, the peripheral areas of the rich countries are crying out for it. But it turns out that no, you cannot have mini-plants because people have got it in their heads that there's only *one* kind of cement—Portland cement—and that it can be made efficiently only on a large scale. The precise process of how Portland cement is made is not theoretically understood. Maybe we can try to learn more about it and then we can build the mini-plant. But in this search we might ask the question, Why does it have to be *Portland cement?* Go around Europe, go to Asia, and you'll find the most magnificent, wonderful buildings. The Taj Mahal or the cathedrals of Europe were not made with Portland cement, and they are still standing. Why have we fixed ourselves on Portland cement? Maybe we need Portland cement to build skyscrapers but that is a minority phenomenon. Most buildings are not skyscrapers. What about other cementitious materials? It turns out there are plenty of other materials that can be made into mortar at half the temperature of Portland cement. And for most normal human requirements it is totally adequate and can be made on a small scale. There are similar examples in many different subjects.

But back to Yorkshire. The Yorkshiremen say, Well, we want to participate in this new knowledge. We want to see all these new possibilities. Can we work with you? Never mind whether you work for the developing countries or for England, because of course if we could have small-scale cement and human-scale bricks with very little capital, perhaps even with unconventional sources of energy, because it's on a small scale we can put our unemployed to work and we can look after ourselves. This has also spread to Europe. It has already happened—still very small, and very beautiful—in the United States. Of course, the United States is so huge that there is room for growing points all over the place. What is happening the world over is that on this level of technology, this type of thinking, there are very many lonely plowmen. But what is happening is that the network is gradually coming into being. So that we can share experience, there are now around the world about twenty such groups and they are full of enthusiastic people who have shed their prejudices and see that adjustment to the new situation is not only desirable, it is possible. It is not only possible, but it is in fact quite low cost.

I will end with an example from my recent experience. I know the original inventor of chipboard. He is German and his name is Max Himmelheber, which means "heaven lifter." Max is a delightful man; now that he is in his seventies, with no offspring, he says, This much I need for myself, that I don't need. He set up the Himmelheber Foundation and then came to me wanting my ideas about what to do with the money. He thought in real terms and he was very worried: he listened to my prognosis about fuel supplies and he then wanted to give all his money to set up an institute, as if we need yet another institute. Well, they should study everything, how can things be done by the chaps themselves without vast capital? But, I said, if you try to study everything you study nothing. Start from where you are. You are a wood expert and the kind of chipboard plants you are building all over the world are monsters with an average capacity of one thousand tons a day and a capital cost that is out of this world. There is no future for that. What we need is a mini chipboard plant. Local production from local resources for local use. Why don't you design it? You're the best man to do it. And suddenly he saw something. He understood it. Like scales falling off his eyes. Yes, he said, I can see it. Tiny ones all over the place. Great fun. No problem of management. A man and a boy. Like egg trays.

So he went to his engineering bureau and he said, I want a design study for a mini chipboard plant. They thought he was off his head. I started at the extreme end; I said, Why not one ton a day? Well, one ton a day didn't quite work but 6½ tons a day did. The thing nearly failed; they told me with authority and knowledge that it couldn't be done. The verdict was, You don't understand anything about making chipboard, now pipe down. I listened very carefully. At the end of it you have to have a whopper press in order to recompound the fiber. And with one ton a day, or small production, you could never amortize the press—and then, thank God, they added, required to make the standard-size board. I heard that. I said, *What* size board? Well, the standard size, eight feet. So I said, What size *can* you make? And now we have a design study by these absolutely top experts, not the standard-size board but a board good enough for any man purposes.

All these small ventures may not have much weight at present but they are making a viable future visible in the present.

5. Education for Good Work

It is possible to discuss meaningfully the subject of good work (or education for it) only by first clarifying the questions What is man? Where does he come from? What is the purpose of his life?

I know, of course, that such questions are called "pre-scientific": There is nothing like them in modern physics and most of biology, says the modern scientist, and he is quite right. Maybe he thinks the question What is man? should be answered: Nothing but physics and biology. If this were true there would be no point in discussing "education." If the question "What is man?" is called pre-scientific, this can mean only that science is not of essential importance for the conduct of human life: good answers to pre-scientific questions are infinitely more important.

What can be the meaning of "education" or of "good work" when nothing counts except that which can be precisely stated, measured, counted, or weighed? Neither mathematics nor geometry, neither physics nor chemistry can entertain qualitative notions like good or bad, higher or lower. They can entertain only *quantitative* notions of more or less. It is easy, therefore, to distinguish between less education and more education, and between less work and more work, but a *qualitative* evaluation of education or of work . . . ? How could that be possible? This, we are told, would be *purely subjective;* it could not be *proved;* it would be anybody's guess since it cannot be measured and thus be made objective.

The Cartesian Revolution has removed the vertical dimension from our "map of knowledge"; only the horizontal dimensions are left. To proceed in this flat-land, science provides excellent guidance: it can do everything except lead us out of the dark wood of a meaningless, purposeless, "accidental" existence. Modern science answers the question What is man? with such inspiring phrases as "a cosmic accident" or "a rather unsuccessful product of mindless evolution or natural selection" or "a naked ape," and it is not surprising that it has no answer to the question of what this absurd, accidental product of mindless forces is supposed to do with itself, that is to say, what it should do with its *mind.* (Modern science has much to say about what to do with the body of the unfortunate being: "Survive as best you can!")

What, in these circumstances, can be the purpose of education? In our own Western civilization—as in all other great civilizations—purpose used to be to lead people out of the dark wood of meaninglessness, pur-poselessness, drift, and indulgence, up a mountain where there can be gained the truth that makes you free. This was the traditional wisdom of all peoples in all parts of the world. We modern people, who reject traditional wisdom and deny the existence of the vertical dimension of the spirit, like our forefathers desire nothing more than somehow to be able to rise above the humdrum state of our present life. We hope to do so by growing rich, moving around at ever-increasing speed, traveling to the moon and into space; but whatever we do in these respects, we cannot rise above our own humdrum, petty, egotistical selves. Education may help us to become richer quicker and to travel further faster, but everything remains as meaningless as before. As long as we remain entrapped in the metaphysics represented by the Cartesian Revolution, education can be nothing but a training which, we hope, may enable people to establish themselves more comfortably—the body, not the soul!—in the dark wood of meaningless existence.

In other words, as long as we persist in our arrogance, which dismisses the entirety of traditional wisdom as "pre-scientific" and therefore not to be taken seriously, fit only for the museum, there is no basis for any education other than training for worldly success. Education for good work is quite impossible; how could we possibly distinguish good work from bad work if human life on earth has no meaning or purpose? The word "good" presupposes an aim; good for what? Good for making money; good for promotion; good for fame or power? All this may also be attained by work which, from another point of view, would be considered very bad work. Without traditional wisdom, no answer can be found.

What, then, would traditional wisdom have to say? It

would derive all answers from its knowledge of the task and purpose of human life on earth.

The human being's first task is to learn from society and "tradition" and to find his temporary happiness in receiving directions from outside.

His second task is to interiorize the knowledge he has gained, sift it, sort it out, keep the good and jettison the bad. This process may be called "individuation," becoming self-directed.

The third task is one which he cannot tackle until he has accomplished the first two, and for which he needs the very best help he can possibly find. It is dying to oneself, to one's likes and dislikes, to all one's egocentric preoccupations. To the extent that a person succeeds in this, he ceases to be directed from outside, and he also ceases to be self-directed. He has gained freedom or, one might say, he is then God-directed. (If he is a Christian, that is precisely what he would hope to be able to say.)

If this is the task before each human being, we can say that "good" is what helps me and others along on this journey of liberation. I am called upon to "love my neighbor as myself," but I cannot love him at all—except sensually or sentimentally—unless I have loved myself sufficiently to embark on this good work of development.

How could I love and help my neighbor as long as I have to say, with St. Paul: "My own liberation baffles me. For I find myself not doing what I really want to do but

115

doing what I really loathe"? In order to become capable of doing good work for my neighbor as well as for myself, I am called upon to love God, that is, strenuously and patiently to keep my mind straining and stretching toward the highest things, to levels of being above my own: only there is goodness to be found.

This is the answer given by traditional wisdom, that is to say, by the metaphysics that has given rise to all the great civilizations. From it we can derive all the guidance we need. What are a human being's greatest needs? As a spiritual being, he is primarily and inescapably concerned with values; as a social being, he is primarily and inescapably concerned with other people and also with other sentient creatures; as a person, he is primarily and inescapably concerned with developing himself.

Accordingly—as, I suggest, anyone can confirm from his own experience—there are three things healthy people most need to do and education ought to prepare them for these things:

To act as spiritual beings, that is to say, to act in accordance with their moral impusles—*Man as a divine being.*

To act as neighbors, to render service to his fellows—*Man as a social being.*

To act as persons, as autonomous centers of power and responsibility, that is, to be creatively engaged, using and developing the gifts that we have been blessed with—*Man himself and herself.*

In the fulfillment of the human being's three fundamental needs lies happiness. In their unfulfillment, their frustration, lies unhappiness.

In a subtle way, modern society has made it increasingly difficult or even impossible for most of the people most of the time to meet these needs. And "education," including "higher education," seems to know little about them. Strange to say, most people do not even know what these needs are. For reasons well known to traditional wisdom, human beings are insufficiently "programmed." Even when fully grown, they do not move and act with the sure-footedness of animals. They hesitate, doubt, change their minds, run hither and thither, uncertain not simply of how to get what they want, but uncertain, above all, of what they want.

If education is unable to teach them what they want, is it of any use? Questions like What shall I do with my life? or What must I do to be saved? relate to *ends,* not merely to means. No technical answer, such as Tell me precisely what you want, and I shall teach you how to get it, will do. The whole point is that I do not know what I want. Maybe all I want is to be happy. But the answer, Tell me what you need for happiness, and I shall then be able to advise you what to do, again will not do, because I do not know what I need for happiness. Perhaps someone says, For happiness you need the truth that makes you free—but can the educator tell me what *is* the truth that makes us free? Can he tell me where to find it, guide me to it, or at least point out the direction in which I have to proceed? Maybe I feel that good work is what I am really longing for. Who can tell me what good work is and when work is good?

Traditional wisdom teaches that the function of work is at heart threefold: (1) to give a person a chance to utilize and develop his faculties; (2) to enable him to overcome his inborn egocentricity by joining with other people in a common task; and (3) to bring forth the goods and services needed by all of us for a decent existence.

I think all this needs to be *taught*.

What is the current teaching with regard to *work*? I do not quite know, but, at least until quite recently, I heard it said everywhere that the real task of education was not education for work, but education for leisure. Maybe this extraordinary idea has now been abandoned. Fancy telling young and eager souls, "Now, what I really want you to envisage is how to kill time when you have nothing useful to do."

As our ancestors have known (it has been expressed by Thomas Aquinas), there can be no joy of life without joy of work. This is a statement worth pondering. Laziness, they also know, is sadness of the soul. This, too, is worth pondering. A nineteenth-century thinker said something like this: Just watch it a bit. If you get too many useful machines you will get too many useless people. Another statement worth pondering.

The question is raised: How do we prepare young people for the future world of work? and the first answer, I think, must be: We should prepare them to be able to distinguish between good work and bad work and encourage them *not to accept* the latter. That is to say, they should be encouraged to *reject* meaningless, boring, stultifying, or nerve-racking work in which a man (or woman) is made the servant of a machine or a system. They should be taught that work is the joy of life and is *needed* for our development, but that meaningless work is an abomination.

A sensitive British worker wrote this:

> It is probably wrong to expect factories to be other than they are. After all, they are built to house machines, not men. Inside a factory it soon becomes obvious that steel brought to life by electricity takes precedence over flesh and blood. The onus is on the machines to such an extent that they appear to assume human attributes of those who work them. Machines have become as much like people as people have become like machines. They pulsate with life, while man becomes a robot. There is a premonition of man losing control, an awareness of doom.

It is probably wrong to expect, he says, good work. He has been conditioned not even to expect it! He has been conditioned to believe that man himself is *nothing but* a somewhat complex physico-chemical system, *nothing but* a product of mindless evolution—so he may *suffer* when machines become like men and men become like machines, but he cannot really be surprised or expect anything else.

It is interesting to note that the modern world takes a lot of care that the worker's body should not accidentally or otherwise be damaged. If it *is* damaged, the worker may claim compensation. But his soul and his spirit? If his work damages *him,* by reducing him to a robot—that

119

is just too bad. Here we can see very clearly the crucial importance of metaphysics. Materialistic metaphysics, or the metaphysics of the doctrine of mindless evolution, does not attribute reality to anything but the physical body: why then bother about safety or health when it comes to such nebulous, unreal things as soul or spirit? We acknowledge, and understand the need for, the development of a person's body; but the development of his soul or spirit? Yes, education for the sake of enabling a man or woman to make a living; but education for the sake of leading them out of the dark wood of egocentricity, pettiness, and worldly ignorance—at the most, this would be a purely private affair: does it not smack of "copping out" and "turning one's back on reality"? Materialistic metaphysics, therefore, leaves no room for the idea of good work, *that work is good for the worker.* Anyone who says, "The worker needs work for the development and perfection of his soul," sounds like. a fanciful dreamer, because materialistic metaphysics does not recognize any such need. It recognizes the needs of the body; that they can be met only by somebody's work is an unpleasant fact and perhaps automation will soon abolish it. Meanwhile, the work needs to be done. Let's get on with it, but make sure the body doesn't get hurt.

If we see work as nothing but an unpleasant necessity, it is no use talking about good work, unless we mean *less* work. Why put any goodness into our work beyond the absolute minimum? Who could afford to do good work? What would be the point of making something perfect when something imperfect would do as well? Ananda

Coomaraswamy used to say: "Industry without art is brutality." Why? Because it damages the soul and spirit of the worker. He could say this only because his metaphysics is very different from that of the modern world. He also said: "It is not as if the artist were a special kind of man; every man is a special kind of artist." This is the metaphysics of good work.

How, then, could there be education for good work?

First of all, we should have to alter the metaphysical basis from which we proceed. If we continue to teach that the human being is *nothing but* the outcome of a mindless, meaningless, and purposeless process of evolution, a process of "selection" for survival, that is to say, the outcome of nothing but *utilitarianism*—we only come to a *utilitarian* idea of work: that work is *nothing but* a more or less unpleasant necessity, and the less there is of it the better. Our ancestors knew about good work, but we cannot learn from them if we continue to treat them with friendly contempt—as pathetic illusionists who wasted their time worshiping nonexisting deities; and if we continue to treat *traditional wisdom* as a tissue of superstitious poetry, not to be taken seriously; and if we continue to take materialistic scientism as the one and only measure of progress. The best scientists know that science deals only with small isolated systems, showing how they work, and provides no basis whatsoever for comprehensive metaphysical doctrines like the doctrine of mindless evolution. But we nevertheless still teach the young that the modern theory of evolution is part of science and that it *leaves no room for divine guidance or design,* thus wantonly creating an apparent conflict be-

121

tween science and religion and causing untold confusion.

Education for good work could then begin with a systematic study of traditional wisdom, where answers are to be found to the questions What is man? Where does he come from? What is the purpose of his life? It would then emerge that there is indeed a goal to be reached and that there is also a path to the goal—in fact, that there are many paths to the same summit. The goal can be described as "perfection"—be ye therefore as perfect as your father in heaven is perfect—or as "the kingdom," "salvation," "nirvana," "liberation," "enlightenment," and so forth. And the path to the goal? *Good work.* "Work out your salvation with diligence." Don't bury your talents and don't let anybody else bury them. He who has been given much, of him much will be demanded. In short, life is some sort of school, and in this school nothing counts but good work, work that ennobles the product as it ennobles the producer.

In the process of doing good work the ego of the worker disappears. He frees himself from his ego, so that the divine element in him can become active. Of course, none of this makes sense if we proceed from the basic presuppositions of materialistic scientism. How could the product of mindless evolution, whose abilities are only those selected by blind nature for their utilitarian value in the universal struggle for survival—how could such a product of chance and necessity free itself from its *ego*, the center of its will to survive? What a nonsensical proposition! And the assumption of the existence of a divine element in man is, of course, entirely pre-scientific!

"The world of work," as seen and indeed *created* by this modern metaphysics, is—alas!—a dreary place. Can higher education prepare people for it? How do you prepare people for a kind of serfdom? What *human* qualities are required for becoming efficient servants, machines, "systems," and bureaucracies? The world of work of today is the product of a hundred years of "de-skilling"—why take the trouble and incur the cost of letting people acquire the skills of a craftsman, when all that is wanted is a machine winder? The only skills worth acquiring are those which the system demands, *and they are worthless outside the system.* They have no survival value outside the system and therefore do not even confer the spirit of self-reliance. What does a machine winder do when (let us say) energy shortage stops his machine? Or a computer programmer without a computer?

Maybe higher education could be designed to lead to a *different* world of work—different from the one we have today. This, indeed, would be my most sincere hope. But how could this be as long as higher education clings to the metaphysics of materialistic scientism and its doctrine of mindless evolution? It cannot be. Figs cannot grow on thistles. Good work cannot grow out of such metaphysics. To try to make it grow from such a base can do nothing but increase the prevailing confusion. The most urgent need of our time is and remains the need for *metaphysical reconstruction,* a supreme effort to bring clarity into our deepest convictions with regard to the questions What is man? Where does he come from? and What is the purpose of his life?

6. The Party's Over

In the beautiful hills of Surrey, where I live, you can go for walks, and even on a Sunday you never meet anybody, though you may hear the distant roar of traffic down to the coast. And the story goes that an economist went there for a Sunday-afternoon walk, and he met none else than God Almighty, which gave him a bit of a shock, and he didn't know what to say. He remembered that as a little boy he had been told that what is a thousand years to us is but a minute to the Lord. And he asked Him "Is this so?" and the Lord said, "Yes, this is quite so." By that time he had recovered his composure, and he said to Him, "Then perhaps it may also be true that what is a million pounds to us is only a penny for you." And the Lord said, "Yes, that's quite true." And he said, "Well, Lord, give me one of those pennies." The Lord said, "Certainly, my dear chap. I don't happen to have it on me, but just wait a minute while I fetch it."

And so it is with the salvation expected from the growth of GNP: just wait another minute and we shall all be rich and happy. This notion is becoming increasingly questionable. It's an awesome view one takes from outside the United States, GNP-wise the most successful country of the world, unbelievably high gross national product, and, to put it mildly, a country with problems. A country with poverty, indeed a country with degrees of poverty that many other countries at a much lower GNP are not experiencing. I'm not saying this in a spirit of criticism, but simply in analysis. After all, the Western Europeans are pursuing the same aims; they're only less successful Americans.

To me, this concept of GNP means nothing at all. I know, for certain technical reasons of managing certain money flows in the economy, it may be quite useful; but as a measurement of any kind of achievement to me it's meaningless. Because it's a purely quantitative concept. Statistics don't have to be accurate; they have to be significant. My theory has always been that figures don't mean anything if you can't make them sing. How can anybody assert that "growth" is a good thing? If my children grow, this is a very good thing; if I should suddenly start growing, it would be a disaster. Therefore, the qualitative discrimination is the main thing; it's far more important than some mysterious adding-up of everything. We've all learned at school that you must add together only things of essentially the same quality. So you can't add together apples and the number of evenings spent watching television; this is meaningless. Let's look at the qualitative aspect of the whole matter. Surely our job is always to make up our minds what's good and do our best to let the good grow; and to make up our minds what is evil or not so good and try to diminish it. Whether the two processes, put together, mean a new growth or a net diminution shouldn't interest anyone. The quality of life—not the quantity—yes, that's what matters. GNP, being a purely quantitative concept, bypasses the real question: how to enhance the quality of life.

If you take the world distribution of income, you get very, very many people extremely poor, very many people extremely rich, hardly anybody in the middle. This is a pathological distribution. That is to say, there is not one world anymore. Even on that humble level any semblance of unity has been lost. This applies not only as between the rich countries and the poor countries, where it applies in a horrifying form; it also applies inside many societies. All the developing countries are evermore becoming dual societies with a lot of people immensely poor, a few people immensely rich, and nothing in the middle.

Some people don't observe the idea that they have purposes in life other than the material. To put it in the shorthand of Christian language, their job is really to save their souls and they are using far more of the material means than is necessary for this purpose, and it's most likely that therefore they are greatly hindered. So we see that the rich society, that is, the very few people at the rich end, cannot possibly be a model for the world as a whole, and unless we find a new model we are just going to drift deeper and deeper into disaster. The question is, Is there another pattern that would make life really worth living? These patterns have existed and they have produced some of the greatest works of art and culture that we know of. And they were produced in a culture of poverty, not in a culture of affluence.

What is the culture of poverty? It seems to me that it is a culture in which a very firm distinction is made between two categories of goods, which I shall call the ephemeral goods on the one hand, goods produced in order that they should be destroyed, and eternal goods—perhaps eternal is too big a term—goods which are not to be destroyed, on the other hand. They may be destroyed by accident, but that's not their purpose. In all real cultures the eternal goods were outside the economic cultures, because, after all, how can you calculate eternity? When they built a cathedral, they didn't budget it, they said, "Only the best is good enough. Only that which can be offered to the glory of God is worthy of the dignity of man." But when they came to ephemeral goods they lived frugally.

I visited Florence a year ago for the first time. Opposite this fantastic cathedral there is the statue of the architect, and on the pedestal is the Latin inscription, which, with the greatest difficulty I deciphered. It said, "This is Arnolfo, who, instructed by the municipality of Florence to build a cathedral of such splendor that no human genius can ever surpass it. On account of the superlative endowment of his mind he proved equal to this gigantic task." Instructed, you see. Outside the cathedral are the famous bronze doors by Ghiberti, and you learn that it took him twenty-eight years to do them. There was no patronage behind it; no economist calculated that if these bronze doors were made in twenty-five years instead of twenty-eight, the tourist trade would be increased by three years. The tourist trade has increased by 3000 percent; you can hardly see the doors now, but that is another matter.

The moment we allow the economic calculus to invade everything, then nothing becomes worthwhile anymore. I tried to imagine what it would look like if I found the statue of the architect opposite one of the high-rise office-block buildings in London. It would probably read, "This is Mr. R. W. Smith, member of the Royal Institute of British Architects, who, instructed by the Greater London Council to create an office block of such superlative cheapness per square yard, per square foot, that no human genius can ever underbid it, on account of his superb endowment with computers proved equal to this mean task."

Our problems are so serious that the best way to talk about them is lightheartedly. All we can hope is that, with the many improvements that are really beginning and trying to get us straight, we should not dissipate our powers by neglecting the strength of science and technology. What is needed is a redirection of them, making use of the best stock, and not wasting too much time in being heroic and reinventing the wheel. Get organized, make the best use of people, even those who are not like-minded, who are just as jittery about the future as anybody else, but who can help you.

There are three ways to develop a new intermediate technology. One way is to take the existing very low-level technology and say simply, look, this can be upgraded. It can be done much better, and if one has the eye for it, one finds it can be enormously improved with virtually no capital investment. That's one way, upward.

Another way is to say, Well, now here we make this marvelous equipment but our production processes are designed mainly to save labor. But this machinery is not suitable for poor countries. Let's, in a sense, downgrade it, to fit it into the condition of the developing country.

The third way is to conceive it anew, to lay on design studies after one has conceived the right question. To get the peasants of the developing countries to do this themselves is very difficult; in most cases they just do not have the resources to do it. They have fewer scientists. That's the tragedy. Where a country does swing around and say, Now we want to work on our own problems, which has happened to some extent in a country like Ghana, all things become possible. But too many are looking to Imperial College, London, or Cornell or MIT, instead of attending to the problems of their own country. You don't get much innovation, much real reconsideration of technology, from the developing countries. You don't get *much,* but there is still quite a lot, taking the world as a whole, and therefore one of the most important activities to be undertaken—and we are undertaking it with our slender resources—is to survey the world and see what already exists and evaluate it and perhaps test it. The Filipinos have some absolutely excellent, very simple equipment for rice culture, and so have the Japanese. We see if that equipment is suitable for other conditions and, if it is, make it available.

Now we come to a definition of the whole thing. It's a funny thing how the word, the concept, which is merely a label attached to some intuition, some knowledge, then becomes the thing itself. The Buddhists have a nice expression, that Buddhism is the finger pointing at the moon. The moon is the thing, Buddhism simply directs your attention to it. So a phrase like "appropriate technology" or "intermediate technology" is simply a finger pointing at the moon. And the moon can't be fully described; it can be pointed out in terms of specific situations.

I was asked in the early 1960s to go to India. I didn't know what to do about rural India, but I traveled the whole country, by every conceivable conveyance or nonconveyance, and finally I came back to Delhi and wrote them a little memorandum about it and they assembled all the planners for a two-day seminar. I said, The question that must be raised is, what is the appropriate technology for rural India? The answer, to the best of my insight, is an intermediate technology, something much better than the hoe and much cheaper and easier to maintain than the tractor plow. So, if I make myself understood, intermediate is an answer. At first I got a very bad reception and I left in a huff. But fifteen months later they arranged an all-India conference on intermediate technology. (They still didn't like the term so they called it appropriate technology. That's all right, it's a purely formal term, it makes my life very easy: when I come to India and somebody, as happened quite recently, comes to me and says, Oh, Mr. Schumacher, I don't believe in appropriate technology, I just look him straight in the face and say, Oh, that's splendid. Do you believe in inappropriate technology?)

To determine what precisely is appropriate is pretty difficult, but it has to fit the particular situation. Normally in the rural areas markets are small and the big mass-production units don't fit, so one of the subsidiary definitions is probably that it will be a small unit. I've recently been to Sri Lanka and they told me, We have little sugar estates all over the place but have only one big sugar refinery. To take all the cane into that one place now, with oil costs, transport costs, is uneconomic. Where can we get mini-plants? They had inquired all over the world. They decided that no one had such a plant; the "big system" is not interested. In fact, the mini-plant for sugar refining, just the thing Sri Lanka needs, has been developed in India against the opposition of the large-scale sugar industry. Now that it exists, everybody says, Thank God it exists; now the little people of Sri Lanka and other places have a chance of making a living.

The second point, perfectly obvious, is that in rural areas—poor countries—we do not have an intellectual infrastructure so that we have only to whistle and there comes your manager, top engineer, lawyer, etc. The appropriate technology at the intermediate level will be simple enough that you don't have to have these specialists.

To illustrate, let's say you set up a factory, making anything, in the desert. You find it very much more difficult than setting up a factory in, say, Denver. Why? Because in the desert there is no infrastructure, that is to say, you'll have to build the roads, you'll have to bring the people nearer the factory. You'll have to build the houses for these people, you'll have to build schools for the people, and hospitals, etc., etc. You can't walk out the front door of the factory because you have an accountancy problem and around the next corner you find a first-class accountant. You've got to maybe fly him from thousands of miles away. If you need a new personnel manager you can't, as you can in Denver, just put an advertisement in the local paper and you immediately get twelve applicants. So all those things that are givens when you do it in Denver, that you don't have to bother about, but not givens out in the desert, that is called infrastructure. The infrastructure in many places has accumulated over the years, several generations, and in the European countries for hundreds of years. It includes an immense number of wires and tubes and pipes beneath the roads. If they have to be created in a poor country, in a hurry, they're immensely expensive. Each mile of road can run into millions of dollars. So if you have to have an elaborate infrastructure first and then a mass-production industry, you have to wait a long, long time and I don't know where the wealth would come from to build this elaborate infrastructure. But if you have small-scale it doesn't require an elaborate infrastructure and you can become productive quickly and then perhaps later you will have the wealth to make the infrastructure a bit more elaborate. That's all I mean.

In Burma I found the Buddhists, Burmans like it if one speaks in parables. And I said, Well, you know, there's a road and from the road there's a path and by the path there's a shed. And in the shed is a hen that lays an egg. Well, now, all that—the road, the path, the shed, the hen—is not what you want. You want only that one egg. If you spend all your money on the road, the path, and the shed, you're then broke and can't even have a hen to lay an egg; it's not very good business. So you want to minimize the infrastructure requirement; you want to produce in such a way and at such a location that you don't have to spend all your money on roads, paths, sheds, and the like, and you can spend more money on getting more hens to lay more eggs.

Third, since we are dealing with poverty and not with rich people, it's useless to go to them with some extremely expensive apparatus, wonderful as it may be, and say, Please get out of my way and I'll show you how to do things, which means I'll show you what you can do when you're rich. The poor watch it with increasing astonishment and say, Well, we're not rich so it means nothing to us. It just proves to us that we are nothing. It destroys people. It's what we call, in high-falutin language, a negative demonstration effect. Then we can go home and talk about the culture gap and how we can close it. Intermediate technology says, No, if I want to help I must be genuine about it and become a poor man myself to understand it, and then I quickly realize what fits. Certainly it must be something which can be done without this great capital intensity. Please notice I am not saying that it can be done labor intensively, I am not aiming at that, but rather at capital *saving*. They are very different things. I have no one who enters the situation imaginatively and feels that he wants to do useless labor, so labor intensity as such is not desirable. But capital saving is desirable.

These are some of the criteria that come only gradually into one's mind, and because the child has to have a name we call it intermediate technology. It's a difficult approach because the aid givers, who are they? Basically they are townies, but the problem can be solved only in the rural areas and the gap between townie and country folk is immense. They are, in a manner of speaking, educated and they try to help people who, according to their criteria, are less educated. The gap between the educated and the uneducated is enormous. And thirdly they are rich and they are trying to help the poor and the gap between rich and poor is also enormous. So there are three big chasms to be bridged, which requires extreme effort of the imagination, at which we, the rich countries, the aid-giving countries, have been very poor. We said, We have the answer, now get out of the way and we'll implement it.

Here is a really symbolic example of simple technology that can serve as a symbol for the whole thing, about a different way of thinking. Much of the third world is arid country, not because it doesn't rain, but because the rainwater flows off into the rivers and down into the sea for certain reasons. The Lord has arranged it so that by and large it rains everywhere; there are few places that are exceptions. In some places, like England, it rains all the time; in other cases it comes in great big blobs, and when it comes in great big blobs it runs off the soil very quickly unless you are very careful. Now don't let it run down to the river and out to sea, and say, "Oh, we've got that marvelous technology, we'll build a desalination plant." Even if you do it, you still have fresh water only in one place when it's wanted all over the country. You want the water when you want it—*that* is the thinking. Don't be misled by the marvelous things we do; do the necessary things. Give your intelligence to the construction, for instance, of underground rainwater tanks. Of course we know how to do it expensively. How can we do it cheaply? How can we do it so that the actual expenditure the villager has to make for materials he doesn't have is minimized? Maybe he has to put in a lot of labor. But in many of these countries there's a great surplus of labor. That is appropriate technology, as an example.

I'll give you another example. In order to have efficient oxcarts, the wheels ought to have steel rims. We've forgotten how to bend steel accurately except with big machines in Pittsburgh or Sheffield. How do you do it in a small rural community? Is it beyond the wit of man to do this on a small scale? No, we remember that our forefathers knew how to do it before James Watt, and they had a most ingenious tool. We found one of those tools in a French village, more than two hundred years old—brilliantly conceived, clumsily made. We took this to the National College of Agricultural Engineering in England and said, "Come on, boys, you can do better than that. Upgrade it, use your best mathematics to work out the required curvature and whathave you." The upshot of it is that while hitherto in the modern world the smallest instrument to do this bending job would cost something on the order of £ 700, and require outside power and electricity to operate, this tool upgraded to the level of knowledge of 1974 can be made by the village blacksmith. It costs £7, it doesn't require electricity, and anyone can do it. Now this is something quite different from going back into the preindustrial era. It is using our knowledge in a different way, and we know it can be done.

I emphasize our interest in nonagricultural activities in rural areas. There is only a given amount of land and if the population increases they have to subdivide the land more and more and more. The urgent need is to *bring industry into the rural areas*.

A couple of years ago I went to a place about ninety miles out of Delhi, called Khurja. In the late 1940s the government of India said Khurja is the idea place where we can make our own crockery. We don't have to import it. They set up a pottery development station but nothing happened. The center attracted several first-class technical people. One was Mr. T. N. Sharma, and he realized that nobody had got down to the problem of technology. He persuaded the government to send him around the world to study the technology. He went out as Mr. Sharma but he came back as Dr. Sharma, and immediately he was offered the managership of a big mass-production firm in Calcutta, which he accepted. Suddenly he remembered himself; Good Lord, I was going to help these poor fellows in Khurja. And so he went to Khurja and selected out of all that he had seen the appropriate technology for the little man. Within twelve years, three hundred pottery factories have grown out of the ground like mushrooms.

I was there and found thirty thousand people that are now earning a living from pottery and hospital porcelain and electrical porcelain. It is magic. I was fascinated. Three hundred firms. I moved around and I got hold of a chap who was employing a couple of hundred people. And I said, Where do you come from? He said, I come from the Punjab. Why did you come here? Are you a traditional potter? Oh, no. I come from a farming village. Why did you leave there? No land. My brother's got the land. And where did you learn this? You are running a factory now. I learned it from Dr. Sharma. Well, yes, Dr. Sharma brought you the implements and so on, and trained you, from a technical point of view; but where did you learn management? He said, Learn what? You just manage, he said. Well, I said, you have three hundred people here who come off the farms from little villages and are entrepreneurs employing altogether thirty thousand people. How many go bankrupt here? He said, I've never heard of one. One has to think about this. I have no reason to believe that this totally frank chap was telling lies. I asked other people. We assume that all of this is so extremely difficult because we have created this extremely complex technology. But when it is back to reality, to real simplicity, then management ceased to be a great problem.

Recently I was seated in a restaurant, next to a family of three, a father and mother and a very bright little boy, I would think between eight and ten years of age.

They studied the menu, and the boy said, "Oh, I want liver and bacon." The waitress was there; the father studied the menu, the mother studied the menu, and then the father ordered three steaks. The waitress said, "Two steaks, one liver and bacon," and went off. The boy looked at his mother and said, "Mummy, she thinks I'm real!"

This question, Are we real?, arises particularly in this vast country. I know these situations in industry, when certain people who have been doing the same boring job for a long time are, perhaps by chance, perhaps by way of policy, treated as *people:* and they experience something similar to this little boy. Good Lord, they think, in this place I'm real; I'm not just a means to an end.

Yes, I think you are put into this life with the task of learning to distinguish between that which is really real and really important and permanent and of true value on the one hand, and things trivial, amusing, ephemeral, and of no real value on the other hand. Your intellect has to make that distinction. The world has to attach itself to the things that really matter and not to those ephemeral trivialities which make the most noise. That is the message of religion. I know it is normally handed down in all sorts of other ways, but unless you do that you are an unhappy, messed-up person. It has taken me a long time to discover why Religion has split up into so many different religions; it's so you can choose the one that is the most practical for you. The most practical to me was the Roman Catholic version of Christianity, and now I am relieved of such totally offbeat questions as: How could something incredible, like the human being, have come about by an accidental combination of atoms? So I say, Come off it, this is just stupid. I don't know how it is, but I believe there is a Creator. The moment I believe in this higher level, it would be most improbable that the Creator could have put into life such loquacious beings as you and I and never say a word to us. He has actually communicated to us.

This is called by the simple word "revelation." We have the sacred books of mankind, and having spent many, many years studying them, not only in the Christian tradition, I find that it's the same spirit that is communicating to all of us. By various means, in a subtle way, an educative way. You always have to stretch yourself to understand; it is not meant to be automatic. This is the great education we can receive in life, and once we get hold of that, then suddenly we find that we are no longer worried, we have energy actually to act in this life, we can distinguish between the phony and the real questions, and we're happy.

Our system has been extremely destructive and I think we must get down to the metaphysical or, if you like, the philosophical or religious causes of this situation. We have been hearing lately a great deal of the tragedy of the commons, which shows the metaphysical deterioration from which we are suffering, because as a matter of historical fact, the commons in Western Europe were well looked after. But of course, when this feeling that man is the servant of this world in a sense, or at least a trustee, was organized out of our thinking, then the commons were no longer maintainable. So it is those causes that we have to become aware of. It is quite true that tinkering with the present system has very little effect, except where the tinkering represents a return to the true values. It is of little use to call for a very big change in values without at least incorporating these values in some new structures, no matter how small. Because as we know, or as some of us know, we have been told that in the beginning was the word but then the word must come and become flesh and dwell among us. We are now locked in a crisis of this modern civilization which has given up, more or less, the two teachers that mankind had.

What are these two teachers? One is the marvelous system of living nature: the town civilization is not in touch with that system. And the other one is the traditional values, the traditional wisdom of mankind, which we have also rejected and replaced by some extraordinary structure which we call objective science.

Let us try to utilize this opportunity to recall to our minds what a human person really is. I am saying nothing original, I just remind myself of it. First of all, in some way or another, whatever way you try to express it, he comes from the divine level onto this earth. He is a son or daughter of the divine. Second, he is a social being; he doesn't come alone. He is put into this social context. And third, he or she is an incomplete being. He has been sent here to complete himself. From this insight have been formulated all the ethics and all the instructions to the human race. As a divinely arrived being he is called upon to love God in traditional language. As a social being he is called upon to love his neighbor. And as an incomplete individual being he is called upon to love himself. The social organization ought to reflect these three absolute needs. If these needs are not fulfilled, if he can't do it, he becomes unhappy, destructive, a vandal, a suicidal maniac. The social, political, and economic organizations ought to reflect these needs.

But they do not. Let's take the lowest of the three, namely the need to complete himself with joyful, constructive labor, work, to feel that he is, as a child of God, created. Well, in most jobs he can't do it. Most jobs have been organized to be as dull as anything can possibly be. This is now one of the critical points in many parts of the world because people are no longer prepared to accept it. This is a situation that is still, as it were, cushioned: in some places where you have migrant labor they can still be pushed around. But all that is now finishing. So the kind of industrial trouble that we have in England arises because we don't have a cushion of recent immigrants who will allow themselves to be pushed around. We don't have foreign workers as Germany and many other European countries have and the British are no longer prepared to tolerate certain industrial conditions. They say, You put your thinking cap on and make something that is humane.

The other need, to serve one's neighbor, and the first need, namely to act as a divinely derived being in accordance with our moral impulses, are also frustrated to a very large extent by the size of our organizations. It is only in a small organization that we can meet people face to face and make decisions face to face.

In large organizations all sorts of little people have to implement rules and regulations, and rules and regulations can never be fair. As Thomas Aquinas said, Justice, untempered by mercy, is brutality. Mercy, uncontrolled by justice, is the mother of dissolution. So if you have a big structure you have to have a lot of rules and regulations and the little people who have to deal with the clients and customers and so on. They can't act in accordance with their moral impulses: they say, Oh, I'm sorry, I am here only to execute the rules I am given. I agree, it is most unfair, but I can't do anything about it. So his impulses are frustrated and you get this extraordinary possibility, namely at the top and throughout the ideology of the big thing, the good intentions and the moral people create, because of wrong structuring, an immoral, wicked effect.

I could put it also in another way, which has certain advantages because it embraces the whole of our life, that if the size of the unit is wrong, this means inevitably the eradication to a large extent of T.L.C. Now T.L.C. is the only fertilizer that really works. Don't inquire where you can buy it—you can make it yourself. T.L.C. means tender loving care, and this is what our life needs. When it is organized out of the system, then everything becomes unproductive and madly expensive. Agriculture is a good example of this: through the technological development, the withdrawal of human labor from agriculture, the substitution for T.L.C. of chemicals and big mechanization, we now have a system that has no real future because it is based totally on nonrenewable fossil fuels, and instead of working with nature it bullies nature.

It is very interesting in Britain, time and again our planners will take good agricultural land and build a new council housing estate upon it and then we environmentalists protest that this is an alienation of land and we don't have enough land anyhow. It is criminal to withdraw this land from food production. But three or four years later we find that fifty families have settled on this land, they all have their gardens, and the land produces more than the farm has ever produced. All because the T.L.C. factor has been brought back into it.

Everything is just a matter of the carrying capacity of this earth. There are studies which show that when food production is done on a sort of family scale, intensively, then the output per acre is on the average five times as high as that of a well-run farm. In Britain, where we produce only about half the food that we need, all our modern people—I call them the people of the forward stampede—say, With ever increasing application of chemicals we must double food output. Then they say it is impossible anyhow, yet they now have a plan to increase food output by 3 1/2 percent a year. Actually it is falling by about 7 percent a year. These people are almost unteachable. The question has to be raised, Can we afford agriculture in Britain? I don't think we can really afford agriculture, we can afford only horticulture, where we get really high output per acre, and this requires a new structure.

This is the sort of constructive work that we now have

to do. Getting down to details. We must realize that we are making a bad job today, a very bad job, and we must ask ourselves, How can we make a better job tomorrow? Let us see the abnormality in the things we consider most normal.

This system is wrong; it doesn't work properly. And the further intensification along the same lines is just tripling the case of fanaticism. Fanaticism has been defined as an attitude of redoubling one's efforts when one knows one is on the wrong track. People are worrying their heads about their standard of living when the world around them, where it really matters, is collapsing. I mean, it is not a thing to be taken lightly that in many, many places in the so-called rich world it is really hazardous, even for a man, upstanding, big man, to try to walk home after dusk alone. These are the real things, the gadgets are not real: if I get mugged, that is a real thing.

I will tell you a moment in my life when I almost missed learning something. It was during the war and I was a farm laborer and my task was before breakfast to go to yonder hill and to a field there and count the cattle. I went and I counted the cattle—there were always thirty-two—and then I went back to the bailiff, touched my cap, and said, "Thirty-two, sir," and went and had my breakfast. One day when I arrived at the field an old farmer was standing at the gate, and he said, "Young man, what do you do here every morning?" I said, "Nothing much. I just count the cattle." He shook his head and said, "If you count them every day they won't flourish." I went back, I reported thirty-two, and on the way back I thought, Well, after all, I am a professional statistician, this is only a country yokel, how stupid can he get. One day I went back, I counted and counted again, there were only thirty-one. Well, I didn't want to spend all day there so I went back and reported thirty-one. The bailiff was very angry. He said, "Have your breakfast and then we'll go up there together." And we went together and we searched the place and indeed, under a bush, was a dead beast. I thought to myself, Why have I been counting them all the time? I haven't prevented this beast dying. Perhaps that's what the farmer meant. They won't flourish if you don't look and watch the quality of each individual beast. Look him in the eye. Study the sheen on his coat. Then I might have gone back and said, "Well, I don't know how many I saw but one looks mimsey." Then they would have saved the life of this beast.

There I learned something. I then also found that in all human traditions there has been a very great antagonism against all this counting business. I don't know how many of you still know your Bible, but you can find it in two places, in Chronicles and Kings. The first chap who arranged the census was King David, and when he arranged the census the Lord was utterly furious. He gave him a choice between three penance punishments. And David, said, Yes, yes, I know I have sinned. He didn't argue back. You know, those old Jews used to argue back very freely. He immediately understood there was something wrong in having a census which treats people as if they were units, whereas they are not. Each is a universe.

The Making of Good Work

Peter N. Gillingham

E. F. Schumacher and I met on September 5, 1974, during the first journey he had made across the United States since his days as a graduate student and instructor at Columbia University in the early 1930s.

With the exception of members of his own family, during the last three years of his life I may have spent more time in his company than any other person. Because there is no hotel in the town where he lived in England, I stayed in the Schumacher home for nearly four months between 1974 and 1977. During this time, we chewed over what I and other Americans might best work at to "make a viable future visible in the present" in the North American citadels of industrialized civilization. We also discussed what might go into this book to make it of use to those seeking to do something about the sense of incapacity that infects many people today.

In addition, my colleagues at Intermediate Technology and I had principal responsibility for organizing his later coast-to-coast visits to North America, comprising three weeks in 1975 and six weeks in 1977. In those nine weeks, with two breaks of less than thirty-six hours each, he and I were together constantly.

Many things he said have stayed with me, as the things he wrote tend to ripen in the minds of millions of people as they examine and test them against their reflections on their own experience. This book owes a great deal to his concept that dreaming, thinking, and action—each intersecting with the other two—are the vital components in any human life fully lived. He demonstrated this in his own life and work, and he helped personally to communicate this wisdom to me and to many others: Every one of us has the responsibility and the capability to construct his or her own map of reality and to dream, think, and act on the basis of it—then reflect on the action and its consequences to strengthen and make more fruitful the succeeding cycles of dreaming and thinking and action.

In working on my end of this book, I felt I could do more than just offer my own agenda for how some of Schumacher's insights might be given flesh in such a complex and highly technologized and professionalized society as the United States. So I have come to regard these pages as a way of showing, in a fuller way, the results of working within the penumbra of the Schumacher mind and spirit for three years. His thinking infused my own, and what follows is a testament to his positive impact on a typical confused, hesitant, and self-doubting human being.

The key to this effect lies in the almost universal reaction of people to Small Is Beautiful, *as Schumacher himself reported it. "Almost never would they say, 'Oh, what you have written is so original!' Almost always it would be, 'You know, you said it better than I could, but what you are saying is exactly what I have been thinking all along!' "*

Today we are likely to think of Schumacher as a "social" thinker dealing with vast issues. There is the fact that a book with the subtitle of Economics as if People Mattered *(the phrase came to him in the middle of the night; he thought* Small Is Beautiful *by itself was too simplistic) has to date sold nearly one million copies in the United States alone. And it is true that more and more policy leaders will read him and adapt his thinking to the successive crises that will be hitting us (he thought that after the energy problem, the next two crises—apart from the underlying human/organizational/environmental/resource/technological* problématique*—will be food and health, both separately and together in such phenomena as cancer). But the more I have thought about it, the clearer it has become to me that many of us read Schumacher in an intensely personal way, where we feel a direct one-to-one interaction with him and his mind and spirit. That helps explain the theme and title of this book: the belief that our only salvation individually and collectively lies in taking back the responsibility for finding and creating our own good work, the place where the spiritual and the temporal, the theoretical and the concrete, mankind and nature, all converge; and for increasing our capacities so that we can and will do so.*

E. F. Schumacher died on September 4, 1977. It will be a long time before I can fully understand, much less express adequately, what the intersection of our lives has meant to me. Perhaps it is best simply to reproduce here what I wrote in the stress of the moment soon after his death to some of his other friends on the continent where I live.

Fritz Schumacher used to say, "Perhaps we cannot raise the winds. But each of us can put up the sail, so that when the wind comes we can catch it."

We grieve for his family, and for all of us left behind it means the work will be less fun as we seek to build on the

149

sacrificial investment of energy and time and love he made in all of us.

We rejoice that such a human being lived among us for 66 years, and we rejoice that he was given time to finish A Guide for the Perplexed *and to hold a copy in his hands. And it is good to think that, as he hoists his sail on the next stage of his journey, the winds of heaven are gentle on his face.*

I: Herefords into Brahmas

The year I finished secondary school my eyes started to go bad, and I took a year off before college. My family lived on a ranch in southeastern Arizona. For most of that fifteen-month period I worked for Jim Hathaway, one of several ranchers experimenting in those days after World War II with Brahma (in that country we pronounce it bray-muh) range bulls to breed with their existing mother stock (mostly Hereford with some Angus and a number still showing the Longhorn strain). The advantages of the part-Brahma stock were that they carried more meat on their frames while being able to stand heat better. They could travel longer distances between forage and water, and they were less susceptible to problems like screw worm.

One day we were going to move a herd of twenty or thirty animals higher up in the Huachuca Mountains. As usual we got up two hours before dawn. The others made breakfast and prepared the gear we needed for the day while I, as the youngest, had the job of bringing in the riding horses. This meant searching around in the 4500-acre home pasture until I heard the bells a few of the horses wore around their necks, then herding the remuda back into the home corral.

With the first light coming up behind the peaks to the east, Jim took me aside.

"I know you've worked with regular whiteface stock, but these Brahma-cross breeds are a different kind of animal altogether. With normal stock we'd just turn them out and push them up the canyon, and you'd yell or whistle every so often, slap your lariat against your chaps, maybe pop one on the hind end with your quirt to keep them moving.

"With these critters you can't do any of this. First Scoop opens the gate of the east corral, then he climbs on his horse and rides real slow up the canyon. He doesn't look back, he doesn't speed up or slow down. What we have to do is get the stock to follow him out of curiosity, with maybe one person coming quietly in through the first gate to get behind them and nudge them out gently. Once they move out, the rest of us slide in behind them gentle and quiet and fan out around the drag, just close enough so they'll move ahead because they don't want us that close.

"One or two may want to head up a draw or stop to graze. You ride out around them, never too close, and try to get them to remember where they were going. Never yell, in fact don't talk if you can help it, and never move suddenly or too fast. They have to do things in their own way, and if you spook them even a little bit, they'll scatter up into the brush like a covey of quail. If that happens you can forget about buttoning up your jacket and playing brush popper. They take off cross-country like mule deer, and it'll be two or three days or a week before you even get a look at one of them, and that probably will be in the salt trap."

In that dry country the stock find water, during the months the creeks aren't running, at scattered water holes or cattle tanks fed by a well and windmill. They will walk miles for salt. The ranchers who ran Brahma-cross stock put blocks of salt in large pens, three or four acres in area, with long fencelines converging on the gate like the sides of a funnel. Not long after my conversation with Jim I saw how the salt trap worked.

The gate, made of thick planks bolted to a framework of three-inch steel pipe, was normally left open so that the cattle could come and go freely. On shipping day, with twenty or thirty cattle in the pen, four or five of us gathered on horseback in a clump of trees almost three hundred yards away. Scoop the foreman got down, tied his horse to a tree, and, Smith and Wesson in hand, crawled forward until he was hidden behind a large rock a few yards from the gate.

The rest of us fanned out across the funnel and rode toward the gateway. Normal cattle would have moved away and bunched against the fence on the far side. But these Brahma-cross critters started moving toward us, toward what they knew was the only exit, first walking and then at a trot. Scoop ran forward to close the gate, but as he did two animals sprinted straight toward him. He shot his gun in the air. As they paused, he slammed and barred the gate.

Ordinary fencing is four strands of barbed wire on posts about four feet high placed twelve to twenty feet apart. This pen was built with juniper posts twelve to eighteen inches thick at the butt set eight feet apart, sunk four feet in the ground and tilted outward. The wire was heavy woven hog wire, seven feet high and reinforced with barbed wire. As the gate slammed and the riders approached, three or four of the cattle whirled away from us and ran directly into the fence.

Later, as the stock were being herded up the loading chute into the trailer trucks that would take them to the railhead at Sonoita, Jim saw me straddling the top rail on one trailer, six feet off the floor. I was balancing myself by holding one of the inch-thick steel supports running up the sides of the trailer and across the open top. It was bent askew several inches.

"Better get outside, Pedro. That thing didn't get knocked out of kilter hitting a bridge. You're used to critters that once you get them in a trailer, they stay there. Last year we had a roan steer packed in there with a bunch of others, stood close to six foot high at the withers. He just looked around while we were closing the tailgate, then he reared straight up like a show jumper and climbed out of there. His hind foot hit that crossbeam on the way out. We've seen him a couple of times since then, but he's still out there."

A myth is a story, Claude Lévi-Strauss once wrote, that aims to explain why things are as they are.

For me, the herding of Brahma-cross cattle is a kind of story-myth. It helps me understand some of the puzzling phenomena of the modern world to see that people as a whole are evolving from Herefords into

Brahmas. This process has been visibly under way for several centuries, but the now familiar exponential curve has taken over in the last few generations. It is happening bigger and faster than ever.

Understand that myth is a gross generality. But we might describe Hereford people as relatively stable except when moved to mass action by acute grievances, usually mobilized by charismatic leaders. They are less venturesome, more accepting of the world and their lot, more the led than the leaders, the acted-upon or acted-for rather than the actors.

Brahma people want to think and act on their own initiative. They make their own maps of reality. They tend to resist or question authority, or to create their own patterns of authority. They would rather experience something directly than accept the digested experience of others by way of maxims, laws, or the customary rules of behavior. Today they are especially recognizable for their concern with good work, for having their energies engaged productively in the world in such a way that they feel their work is making them better people.

The Brahma's innate capacities may be greater than the Hereford's—though not by a great deal. But the Brahmas have a fuller sense of their own capabilities, greater confidence in themselves, and a deeper grasp of their potentialities.

In testing the myth against reality, we need to know that in many respects we are looking for evidence of a phenomenon not yet realized as real. Despite the recurrent debate over evolution, nature vs. nurture, individual vs. social evolution, sociobiology, innate vs. acquired characteristics, and the rest of it, we still operate on the assumption that man as genotype is a stabilized species. In other words, people are people.

Various programs and institutions, and how they are designed and operated, may make people more or less content, more or less productive, by what is done to or for them, or not done; this much is familiar to us. But the idea that the basic human capital of the earth, the net average capacities of the people on the planet, may have been changing significantly is still alien to us. Yet fragments of the evidence confront us every day as we observe how people behave and how institutions do or do not seem to serve them well.

Looking for the operative factors that brought this about, an obvious starting point is food and nutrition. "You are what you eat," at least in modern Western cultures, has been understood to mean only that how and what you eat can affect your health or strength or general well-being, rather than that it can affect your fundamental capacities. Yet in the past fifteen years it has become widely known and accepted that when the diet of a child in its first five years of life (or the diet of the mother before birth) has been significantly deficient in protein and particularly some of the amino acids, the individual's intelligence will be impaired, probably permanently. The person does not grow up a moron or cretin, but his or her cognitive capacities and potential for abstract, analytical, or imaginative thinking are dulled and restricted—in terms of our myth, a Hereford.

Throughout most of human history, large civilizations were incapable of providing the great mass of people—maybe as many as 99 percent of them—with a diet adequate in these amino acids that influence and feed brain development and the use of the mind. The most common diet was almost exclusively carbohydrate in the form of such easily stored staples as wheat, rye, beans, corn, cassava, potatoes, soybeans, or rice. There were, of course, more complete sources of protein available, but generally in limited quantities and perishable form. A speculative mind might be intrigued to notice how often the "sumptuary laws" in past civilizations limited the consumption of meat to rulers, priests, and other elites; or how many of the "Golden Age" periods marked by great creativity and widespread social energy—Periclean Greece, Elizabethan England, Meiji Japan—occurred in compact societies with active fishing fleets.

Until some time into the late eighteenth or early nineteenth century, in fact, inadequate diet produced a situation where, in any generation, 90 percent or more of the children reached the starting line of systematic cognitive activity, age five or six, already significantly handicapped.

By then, of course, many other things were starting to happen; or rather, many things that had been occurring accidentally or on a small scale or in isolated circumstances began taking place more visibly. Agricultural production increased in many nations by virtue of selective breeding, mechanization, and artificial fertilizers. The scope and carrying capacity of farm-to-market transportation increased in company with industrialization and urban concentrations. New techniques for preserving and storing perishable foods, supplementing traditional technologies such as salting and smoking and drying, were developed. The result of these changes was that large populations were able to have a diverse diet during most of the year.

Food and nutrition constitute a simple example of the factors feeding the Hereford-into-Brahma shift—if only because it is so easy to comprehend the "down side," the state of relative deprivation that existed continuously throughout human history. With other factors, it is harder to appreciate how deeply they have changed people. But added together, these factors have changed the environment humans inhabit to such a great degree that one must almost think in terms of a different *kind* of people inhabiting the earth today.

Wilder Penfield is the best known of many scientists whose work over the past two generations has indicated that mental activity can actually change people, by changing the structure of the brain—the density, for instance, of the vascular structure in the cortex. These scientists tell us that we have barely reached the letter "B" in understanding the full capabilities of human beings given the right opportunities for experience and for applying, testing, and stretching their powers.

From this perspective, the enormous increase in the amount of sensory stimuli and information available to people must have already begun to produce some widespread qualitative changes in the way people function. The step-up points are familiar: Gutenberg and the development of movable type; in the eighteenth century the proliferation of newspapers; in the nineteenth century the vast increase in individual mobility by water and rail, and. radical improvements in papermaking and printing technologies leading to mass production of cheap books, together with the proliferation of Mechanics Institutes and other free or cheap libraries, as well as debating societies and public lectures and Chautauquas; in the twentieth century the explosive growth of electronic media and computers that have put the world inside everyone's living room.

The proliferation of formal education (to the point that it may interfere with the full exercise of people's cognitive and imaginative capabilities) has undoubtedly been a factor of still incalculable importance. North America, Japan, most of Eastern and Western Europe, and other countries have no guide, no evidence from past history, to help us comprehend the cumulative impact of being in the fourth generation of nearly universal access to primary education, the second generation of similar access to secondary education, and deep in the first generation of very wide access to post–secondary education and training.

Yet there are many other factors that have acted to give more people more raw material for their minds and experience and imaginations to work on—and often provided powerful stimuli to make use of their minds and imaginations. One of these, clearly, is the destabilizing effect of rapid change and greater mobility and communications, which permit or make more people think or worry about more different "things per person." People in this period began to concern themselves with things outside their immediate physical surroundings to a degree their ancestors never had.

Industrialization and all its related social, economic, and political phenomena uprooted people from being tied to (and drawing psychic sustenance from) the land and other types of primary production. The effect was to shift people's minds and hands and spirits from nature and its processes to human artifacts such as industry, cities and their technology, and organizations of increasing complexity. We are aware of many of the negative effects of this; one of the positive (or double-edged) phenomena it brought about was proliferation of different kinds of work and therefore ways in which people had to stretch their capabilities, physical skills, and understanding.

One important aspect of this was the startling increase during the eighteenth and particularly the nineteenth century in the number and activity of various organizations and institutions which created demanding and rewarding *roles* for people.

In 1831 Alexis de Tocqueville was fascinated by the tendency of Americans to form voluntary associations to accomplish whatever needed doing, from putting out fires to schooling children to raising a statue in someone's honor. The important thing about these associations—which had counterparts elsewhere during the next half-century—is that often they involved people who had never before taken initiative or leadership roles beyond the scope of their own family, farm, or workshop.

When institutions such as labor unions and granges are discussed today, we usually think of the sense of excitement and political power people derived as a mass, as a group seeking recognition for common needs and wants. But what may be more important in understanding the present and the future is that the rise of such organizations created thousands of roles that were filled by people who had been considered (and almost more important, had considered themselves) the passive or acted-upon rather than actors or initiators. These roles challenged people to think and act in larger arenas, accepting responsibility for more people and for dealing with more complicated issues and information and wider horizons. Their performance created both in their eyes and in others' a vastly increased sense of the scope of their own capacities and of "common people" in general.

There were two more factors so obvious they are easy to overlook. One might be called simply the "sense of the possible." One difficulty with the four-minute mile or any other new achievement is in the conception itself, the imaging, in imagining with increasing clarity and conviction that it can be done at all. The whole climate of the Western world in the past three or four hundred years represents a break with a past where the majority of people lived with the primary assumption that things would stay as they were. It was not so much that they thought of things which might be possible and decided they couldn't be done; there was simply nothing in the world around them to make the thought of such a possibility enter their minds at all.

In our own day we expect material changes and startling developments to such a degree that moon landings became commonplace in a span of months. But some generations ago the developments associated with new institutions and new technologies and skills created a sense of quickening possibility which was something new on the earth.

Underlying all of these developments were the profound deep-current effects of ideas about the social and political systems within which people could and would function most effectively and happily. Aristotle was the towering spirit of his era, yet he found it natural to write a reasoned justification of slavery. In the Greek *polis* only adult male owners of property were considered people: women, slaves, and children were not.

In some ways it is valid to call the eighteenth through twentieth centuries the "age of ideologies." While democracy, capitalism, socialism, communism, and other competing social ideas were largely focused on the shape and responsibilities of nation-states, they shared an explosive new concept of the total capabilities of human populations in the emerging conditions of the modern world. Capitalism might seem to many today an anomaly in this list, but in a very real way it typified the whole process with its concept of the limited-liability corporation capable of taking new risks and organizing new enterprises.

The political ideologies were primarily concerned with the rights of human beings rather than with their capacities consciously thought of as such. But underlying the entire process was a yeasty slow-rising awareness that people were capable of what they had perhaps not been in the past. When representative democracy was proposed as a form of government in the eighteenth century, in a world which until then had known in large civilizations primarily monarchies or theocracies or tyrannies, it was put forward—in North America particularly—not by romantic theoreticians but by hard-headed people with an extensive knowledge of the everyday world and how it worked.

What speaks through the words and actions of our founding fathers—on which, it is useful to remember, they were staking their lives—was a new myth, or map of reality, substantially at variance with what had been believed about human beings up to that point. There had been much thought and talk about the possibilities of the spiritual evolution of human beings, but not much about possible changes in their actual capacities on this earth: people were people. Now they were saying that there was enough ability and initiative and sense of responsibility, widely enough distributed among the populace at large, to make this daring new system of government work.

II: The Yeast of War

If something like this Hereford-into-Brahma phe-nomenon *is* happening, we can assume it will show up more clearly at a time of social stress, what Arnold Toynbee would call a time of "maximum challenge." For that reason, it may be especially instructive to look at the American experience during World War II, when the society was challenged in a way that produced a maximum response.

I find three phenomena especially striking. When the United States came into the war at the end of 1941, our allies had all been fighting for some months or years and except for Britain and parts of China and the Soviet Union had been overrun by the Axis powers. The industrialized capacity of the United States had to be mobilized quickly to provide material and supplies not merely for our own participation but for the other Allies. Some of these achievements were phenomenal. Where, for instance, we had produced less than five hundred multi-engined bombing aircraft during 1941, it was decided that we must produce twenty thousand during 1942.

If a third of these aircraft were to be ferried overseas immediately to be used by other powers, then we had to find and train in one year, allowing for two pilots per plane plus casualties and replacements, forty-five thousand bomber pilos. At the time, knowledgeable people were working to analyze the hundreds of different jobs involved in carrying on a war with technologies and administrative techniques far more complex than those used a generation before in World War I. Not unreasonably, they decided that flying a bomber as either pilot or co-pilot was sufficiently demanding to require a college graduate. At this point they discovered that in the entire nation, with a population at that time of around 130 million people, there simply did not exist forty-five thousand male college graduates who were also physically qualified to be bomber pilots—and that takes no account of all the other personnel requirements of the army and navy and the whole defense industry, not to mention the civilian economy.

What happened? What could they do? Those involved look back with some wonderment today and say they simply learned in six months what normally took a generation or two. First they developed psychological, intelligence, and aptitude testing techniques so that they could pick tens of thousands of men (many of whom had little formal education beyond grammar school) as suitable for training from among millions of factory workers, schoolboys, soda fountain attendants, farmers, and bookkeepers. And simultaneously they developed training procedures by which these people could be turned into competent bomber pilots within six to nine months.

It worked, and everyone went on to the next job. Amid the exhaustion of hundred-hour weeks a few people stopped to reflect that what had been accomplished seemed to fly in the face of what was known or had been thought to be true about the average capabilities of human beings in the mass. But most of them attributed it to the "adrenaline rush" affecting millions of people all over the world fighting for their survival, and promptly forgot about it. Still, some people were alerted by what happened, and from one of them I heard the next story.

During 1942 the three large English-speaking powers moved to mingle their military personnel for training on complex equipment such as anti-aircraft gunnery predictors or submarine detectors. While standardized intelligence tests showed there was little or no difference in average intelligence among the three groups, the Americans taken as a whole learned a bit more quickly than the Canadians, and the Canadians more quickly than the British. This puzzled and bothered a few social scientists enough that they tried to figure out why it was so.

They considered nutrition (though caloric rather than protein intake was their concern in those days), education, employment in various industrial or mechanical pursuits, all without success. Finally they discovered an almost uncanny correlation between the levels of training performance of the three groups and the percentage of the population in each country who before the war had taken out drivers' licenses. To the people trying to understand what was happening, the explanation that made the most sense was that more of the Americans had had a chance to work or play around with different types of complex machinery—the most ubiquitous at that point, in terms of how many people's lives it touched, being the automobile, the Model T in the yard.

Earlier I mentioned the work of Wilder Penfield and others relating to the physical effect on the brain of mental activity. Going beyond this, I suspect that various types of physical activity in which neuromotor capabilities interact with mental processes to strengthen both are the most dangerously neglected components of modern education, given the fact that the rest of life outside the schools no longer provides the challenges and opportunities for young people, in the form of productive work, that once was the case. As James Coleman put it some years ago, life in general used to be experience-rich and stimulus-poor; now it has become nearer the reverse. Yet we do nothing effective either to reopen the wider environment or to change substantially what goes on in education. We have lots of sports and a good deal of plastic and performing arts in education, and more attention paid to the "affective" or the emotional side of things. But the idea that productive work of the right kinds provides the most powerful opportunity for self-education still seems a musty, high-minded slogan from another day. For some people it only evokes the horrors of child labor in the nineteenth century.

In dealing with various forms of *in*capacity we have learned a great deal about how physical, neuromotor activities affect the total individual, including his or her cognitive capabilities and especially the crucial factor of his attitude toward the world around and his sense of his capabilities to cope with it. Less than twenty years ago it was shocking to be told that children with dyslexia and other eye-brain reading difficulties could be brought in a matter of weeks or a few months up to normal performance by putting them down on the floor to crawl on their hands and knees. It is now accepted that fond modern parents were encouraging their children to walk at an age when actually they needed more crawling, a complex activity in which neurological circuits develop in concert with the physical and mental circuitry essential to the body-eye-brain process involved in reading and comprehension.

Yet we are barely beginning to apply this kind of thinking, imaging, and action to "normalcy" and how ordinary people can have more experiences which first suggest and then solidify increased capacities.

The third story concerns the veterans of World War II. I believe the American program for veterans, loosely known as the "G.I. Bill of Rights," will be regarded by history as one of the pivotal socioeconomic events of the twentieth century. Until this century, nearly all wars were fought by professional soldiers. After the war was over, they were perhaps to be thanked and rewarded, but they were thereafter regarded as potentially dangerous gladiators to be disbanded or put back into the cage until needed again.

After World War I, which involved larger percentages of the population of European nations, there was some positive change of attitude. In Britain, for instance, there was a limited program for former officers risen from the ranks to be educated at government expense at Cambridge and Oxford. But on the whole, not much was done for the GIs. In the United States Congress, one of the floor leaders of the legislation to provide mustering-out bonuses for our heroic doughboys advocated that the bonus be paid in three installments rather than one lump sum, so that "they couldn't drink it up all at once."

In 1944, only one generation later, Congress passed legislation that among other things made it possible for almost any veteran to take four years of college education. The legislation was popular with the country at large: partly out of gratitude to the fourteen million people who had served in uniform, partly because of the American love affair with higher education that developed in the middle of the nineteenth century, and partly because it seemed a sensible thing to do with millions of people who would otherwise swell the unemployment rolls.

From the perspective of the Hereford-into-Brahma myth, what interests me most is that at the time this legislation was passed nearly all of the "decision makers" and influential elites in this country were dubious if not deeply worried about the G.I. Bill. Despite the glowing financial prospects it promised for their colleges and universities, many administrators and faculty were disturbed (and said so repeatedly, in the press and professional journals) at the prospect of flooding their campuses with students who would not be able to profit from the opportunities offered them.

The academics soon found that the maturity and drive of the veterans stretched and challenged their own capacities to such a degree that they have since come to regard that generation of veterans as a sort of Golden Age in American higher education.

But the real surprise came in the early 1960s, when the sub-field of economics concerned with "human resource development" showed that the G.I. Bill was dollar for dollar one of the most productive national investments in history. Even then, only fifteen years after most World War II veterans had finished using their educational benefits, the increased income taxes they had paid, compared with the taxes they might have been expected to pay in jobs geared to their prewar educational levels, had already more than covered the entire cost of the G.I. Bill, quite aside from the contributions these legions of better-trained people made to the society and the economy and polity in general.

In terms of our myth, World War II sharply accelerated the evolution of Herefords into Brahmas. Those years radically changed people's views of themselves, their capabilities, their prospects. There was an explosion of new roles and opportunities in the world that challenged people, engaged them, extended them. The result was a significant shift in the human resource pyramid. Nothing has been quite the same since.

III: The Moron Shortage

The idea of a human resource pyramid gives us a graphic way to look at the Hereford-into-Brahma myth. The horizontal represents numbers of people, and the vertical represents their degree and diversity of capacity.

Until fairly recently, the last three or four hundred years, every large civilization displayed a human resource pyramid that looked something like this:

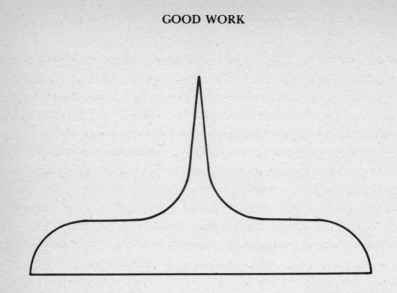

Toward the bottom are the Herefords: the passive, the acted-upon and acted-for, the cannon fodder of civilization. Toward the top are the Brahmas, those who demonstrate initiative and any unusual behavior valued by the society then or later, whether as scholars, generals, mystics, farmers, or tribal weavers inventing new designs. (Note well: those at the top of the pyramid are not necessarily better people in moral or ethical terms than those at the bottom.)

What separates the people at the top from the people at the bottom are their capacities. These are composed of three elements: (a) possessing recognized capabilities; (b) knowing consciously or unconsciously that one has these capacities; (c) having or creating or being forced into a situation where one exercises these capacities, thereby strengthening and expanding them and "realizing" them, making them more real to oneself and others.

Looking at the available evidence, much of the past seems a time when most people had the first characteristic to some degree, lacked the second, and had the third only in times of stress such as war or disaster. By contrast, much of the present makes sense as a time when more and more people have the first and second characteristics but lack the third.

Now let's return to those operative factors mentioned earlier: diet and nutrition, education, everyday contact with stimulating technologies, extended communications, and more challenging roles for people to play. These have all been having their effects for a century or two now, each trend strengthening the others. The cumulative impact has been to reshape the human resource pyramid. The top is still pointed, because the truly extraordinary are still rare, but it is somewhat broader than before. The base of the pyramid has narrowed: there is less of inert mass. In the middle is the most striking change: the width there has pushed the sides much farther out.

Throughout history, once social institutions evolved beyond the tribal or communal stage, the percentage of actors (as compared with the acted-upon or -for) has ranged from a minimum of $1/10$ of 1 percent in a very stagnant or repressive society up to a maximum of 10 percent in some "modern" societies.

Taking only the protein and amino acid dimension of nutrition by itself, we can see how the change has accelerated. In the fifteenth century the capability of

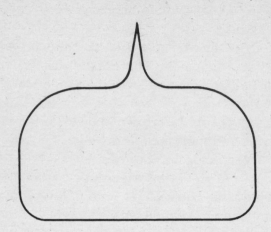

any nation on earth to produce, store, and "deliver" foodstuffs of the right type to its people, was so inadequate that 90 to 99 percent of its population took their places as children at the "starting line" of cognitive intellectual activity with their capacities already significantly stunted or impaired.

By the late nineteenth century, production, storage, preservation, and delivery capabilities had improved to where this figure was reduced to a worldwide average of 85 percent, with some large nations down to a figure of 80 percent or even 75 percent. (And remember, all the other operative factors are strengthening the second two factors involved in "capacity." There is both greater awareness of possibilities and more opportunity to engage them in the world.)

By the third quarter of the twentieth century, despite declining food production and starvation in some parts of the world, the worldwide average is down to around 80 percent, with a number of large nations so prosperous and organized that they are down into the 50 to 30 percent range.

Now turn these figures on their heads. Look at the numbers of those who are *not* impaired mentally. If from the dawn of history 90 to 99 percent of the population of most societies was impaired in imaginative or analytical intelligence, then we have a skewed view of what "normal" human beings are like and what they are capable of. If we take the percentage of *un*impaired people and watch it rise from 1–5 percent to a worldwide average of 20 percent, with a number of large and influential "bellwether" nations rising to 30 or 40 percent or more, and if we add in the reinforcing effect of the other operative factors, then we have a quintupling of the number of people capable of conceptualizing, or communicating, or planning, or acting, or leading others with an unusual degree of initiative, effectiveness, and confidence.

There is an enormous slow upward heave in the mass of mankind measured by the numbers of people beginning to sense that they are capable of directing their own lives, of taking their own initiatives, of formulating roles or rules or operating procedures for themselves rather than having others do it for them, of making their own choices, of assuming increased responsibility for themselves and others as their sense of their own capacities develops. Schumacher spoke pungently of

173

this phenomenon as "the moron shortage." In other terms, many more Brahmas than before. Compared with what we were conditioned by the realities of earlier human history to regard as "normal," what has been happening to the human race, gradually for some centuries and with steadily increasing speed over the past four to six generations, is that we are turning into a race of supermen and superwomen.

IV: The 1000 Percent Revolution

The early stages of the swelling human resource pyramid gave rise to the modern industrialized world. To what degree people's new capacities were the cause or effect of the vast upheavals of two centuries ago is vain to argue; each produced and was produced by the other. But the outcome was almost inconceivable. In the space of a few decades there was a 1000 percent increase in the leadership and initiative activity of the society.

To return to our statistics, until the modern era less than 1 percent of the population was involved in anything other than the routine maintenance functions that enabled the continuation of things as they were. The mass of the population lived in a "scarcity" condition where they had little hope and less opportunity to improve their physical lot. But with the rise of the industrial age, suddenly more like 10 percent of the population was able to engage in active, creative, knowledge-related, non-stasis social roles. The coming of large technology, large science, large and complex organizations, and large professions multiplied quickly the opportunities to invent and innovate, to provide leadership, to exercise creative and ordering capacities, to explore ideas and generate knowledge. The overall expansion of human capital was nearly incalculable.

At today's remove, it is easy to lose sight of what a profoundly liberating influence the growth of large technologies* seemed to hold for human beings. For the 10 percent who were heir to the new opportunities, their lives were transformed. In particular, they were engaged in work roles that were not only stimulating and satisfying on a personal level, but also seemed to improve the lot of the remaining 90 percent. Industrial mass production, massive government public works, sprawling systems of public education, pyramiding medical advances: these were the monuments to having harnessed a radical new degree of human capacity in the world, quite aside from the forces of nature.

Professionalization and specialization offered a special kind of "irresponsibility" (a parallel is the limited-liability corporation) where people in large numbers for the first time were able to experience what had earlier been reserved to a few monks and wealthy aesthetes: relinquishing responsibility for, attention to, and action in many different sectors of life in order to focus in

*Schumacher was always impatient with those who uncritically feared technology and thought of it as only tangible physical hardware. "Technology is how you get something done," he would say. So by large technologies I am referring not only to the new hardware of the time but also to the growth of large-scale organizations, the professions, the emphasis on organized knowledge, the enterprise of corporate science in industry and universities and research organizations, and so forth.

175

depth on a particular slice of life, a single problem or phenomenon, becoming what we know as an "expert." The day-to-day responsibilities that had hemmed in our ancestors were now being taken care of by other specialists (most of them within institutions constantly proliferating in size and diversity) or by hired labor. More per capita income plus more specialized jobs meant a greatly reduced necessity for people to spread their energy and attention across the full spectrum of human needs. You could pay someone else to build a house for you, and you could pay taxes instead of putting in two weeks of labor a year fixing local roads.

The First Revolution was marked especially by the rise of knowledge people. In order of ascending numbers and social influence:

(a) People concerned with the generation of knowledge, such as scholars and research scientists;
(b) People concerned with the storage and retrieval of knowledge, such as librarians, museum curators, computer people, designers and operators of information systems;
(c) People concerned with the transmission of knowledge, such as teachers, writers, magazine editors, and communications specialists; and
(d) People concerned with the application of knowledge to solving problems. This is a classic definition of a professional, whether a doctor or public administrator or sanitary engineer.

Historically these knowledge people were not only small in number but usually the kept retainers of those who exercised temporal power. But following the First

176

Revolution, knowledge people ended up at the levers of power themselves; they became operators and arbiters in power transactions based on real or apparent access to knowledge. This coming to power seemed at the time a perfectly marvelous development. It offered a distinct improvement over most of history when decisions were made by those who held power not on the basis of knowledge (facts, statistics, balancing of costs and benefits, logical presentation on the basis of objective evidence) but on the basis of whim, personal relationships, or a narrowly conceived idea of their own self-interest.

The power exercised by knowledge people resulted in a new set of institutional edifices in the society. There has been a strong continuing trend toward large organizations and large technologies, and toward the orchestration of hitherto fragmented individual efforts within large corporate structures or systems. There has also been a powerful emphasis on the comprehensive and inclusive and standardized over the specific and concrete and localized. These tendencies have been fed by many different kinds of elements. For example:

- Inventions such as Eli Whitney's mass-produced musket, with parts so precisely interchangeable that "new" weapons could be assembled on the battlefield with the parts of damaged ones, helped to bring about a standardized mass production that—the goods it produced quite aside—had a strong stimulating and liberating effect on the public imagination.

- The struggle of the professions to define and strengthen themselves, and to increase the level of competence and integrity in the average practitioner, by setting and enforcing standards of practice and conduct.
- The evolution within large organizations of scientific-appearing, standardized, and seemingly even-handed techniques of management and administration to replace the loose-jointed specific-case techniques of before.
- The aspirations of members of the academic disciplines and professions to explain and predict within an ever-larger framework of universality and the consequent emphasis on methodological rigor and regularity.
- The rise of mass communications, especially national news publications, in order to hold a national audience, emphasized the comprehensive issues of apparent concern to the nation at the cost of local events.
- The spirit of the United States itself, a nation that only with difficulty constituted itself a union of many separate and previously independent parts, and whose population and leadership were for generations seemingly obsessed with creating a unified *ethos* transcending all parochial local and ethnic values and allegiances.

The net effect of these and related developments was to provide an enormous sense of adventure, of excitement and liberation, at finally escaping the mire of the particular, the limited, the communal, the immediate, the local.

For the 1 percent-turned-10 percent, the dynamics of the time brought a rare level of personal satisfaction and, one presumes, happiness. In their lives and their sense of themselves, they were moving toward great *individuation* and differentiation from the mass; in their view of the world and their engagement with it, they were always moving toward greater levels of generality and *comprehensiveness*. The two complementary dynamics resulted in a new sense of relationship to the world.

Because they provided so many satisfactions to so many more people, the great professional, technological, and organizational juggernauts developed irresistible momentum. They have carried us into an ever more complex, interdependent, and imperfectly understood set of interrelationships. Only now are we beginning to recognize the human and resource costs exacted by these behemoth dinosaur activities.

Sometimes the problem manifests itself as a matter of excess. The power of knowledge people, which once seemed so bright and so benign, now gives rise to an institutional version of Gresham's Law: Even the most dubious theories or statistics routinely carry the day against clear and compelling human experience. As they say in Washington, "Who's got the best numbers?" We have reached a pass where the knowledge generated by an individual using his or her own brain and judgment on the raw materials of everyday experience (including what we might call common sense and all forms of folk or street knowledge) actually counts for nothing if it is not accompanied by the proper educational credentials and professional, academic, or institutional position.

The government poverty programs of the 1960s show how dependent the social power process has become on professional knowledge handlers. These put a novel emphasis on "maximum feasible participation" by the poor themselves. But more often than not, when poor, uneducated, uncredentialed people were put in positions of real decision-making power, they found themselves frustrated and ineffective because they had not had experience marshaling organized knowledge in the manner that turns the wheels of complex organizations, and keeps them turning inside the multilayered structure of divided authority and accountability. The true power kept gravitating back to the trained administrators, academics, planners, professionals, and civil servants. This was not because the knowledge people secretly wanted it that way—some of them bitterly regretted what they perceived as the "failure" of the poor to justify their high-minded faith in them—but because power and knowledge have become so entangled that they can no longer be manipulated separately.

Other times, problems manifest themselves in the form of unexpected consequences. Huge organizations staffed by numberless specialists may be reaching the limits of their grasp on the world. I recall the great activity formerly in fashion among foreign assistance agencies to build large dams in small African countries—frequently to produce hydroelectric power to process their bauxite deposits into alumina, the industrial raw material for aluminum. Many professionals—planners, engineers, economists, administrators—took great and what seemed at the time perfectly justifiable pride in the huge works that resulted from their labors. A few years later, however, it became apparent that schistosomiasis and related crippling diseases were sharply on the rise, primarily because the organisms that carry them remain under control in the moving currents of natural rivers, but quickly proliferate in large bodies of standing water. Each professional, qua professional, could stoutly and honestly maintain that it wasn't his job to anticipate this ultimate effect; but as human beings they recognized that something was wrong with a system that could with such good will bring about unexpected ill.

Each of us has a private list of examples where professional hubris was confounded by the intransigencies of the world. What is beginning to happen now, however, is that the knowledge people themselves are beginning to sense a crisis. There is a profound self-questioning inside those precincts that flows from a loss of faith and confidence in their abilities, their scope of vision or understanding, and their presumptions. For most professionals, the crisis in its full dimensions is fourfold. It covers their *competence*—how well they do what they do, and especially how well they foresee the longer-range impacts—and their *integrity*—what are the motives with which they do what they do, and especially how much personal responsibility they are willing to take for the consequences of their work. The searching questions are raised on the *inside*—in professional dialogues and amid shoptalk—and on the *outside*—by the public at large and by the worlds of clients and patients and subjects, those specifically for whom and on whom the professionals or their works act.

There is earnest self-questioning in the older "high wall" professions such as law and medicine and the clergy as well as among engineers and city planners. Accountants, to take one example, say their profession is nearly a shambles as they try to sort out just when and where accounting firms have to take an independent line of judgment against the interests of their corporate clients. Similar problems and questions appear among economists in academia and government; among teachers and the professoriate in general; in the media; among leaders and managers of large corporations, universities, and government bureaucracies. It is not only criticism from outside or inside; for many individuals the crucial manifestation of difficulty is their realization that their daily work is simply not as much fun or as satisfying as it once was or as they expected it to be.

The older-generation Brahmas, to put it simply, are feeling the pressures of the swelling human resource pyramid. There may be a four- or fivefold increase in the number of Brahmas. In some places, they may soon outnumber the Herefords.

The sudden weakening of the confidence and momentum of the old 1 percent-turned-10 percent, aided by their new degree of sensitivity, has revealed an important truth: The liberating, exhilarating, self-fulfilling experiences of the 10 percent are generally at the expense of the 90 percent. The 10 percent needs the rest of the population to act on or act for. But the accelerating upward bulge of the human resource pyramid means that the 90 percent increasingly have the capacity and desire to do for themselves what the heretofore happy 10 percent have been busily working on for them. Awareness is spreading that the activities of the 10 percent tend to paralyze, pre-empt, dull, or intimidate the capacities of the rest of the population to do these things for themselves. Thus there is resentment around about professionals who (a) present things on such a large scale and in such complexity that they overwhelm the average person; and (b) send an implicit message that they are the only ones capable of dealing with these issues in their true complicatedness and that the experience, insights, ideas, and actions of the rest of us are irrelevant, trivial, or even possibly damaging.

Another way of stating the matter is this: At the same time that the old 10 percent group is losing its sense of capacity and significance, more of the 90 percent are beginning to find theirs. The continuing Hereford-into-Brahma shift is responsible for more and more people coming to feel that *they have to* and that *they can* perform for themselves knowledge and imaging functions.

Meantime, of course, the old assumptions continue to result in the flow of freshly minted professionals looking for people to operate on. This will only add to the sense of crisis. For me the whole advancing collision is symbolized by the horrifying statistic that in California

(22 million population) forty-four of every thousand adult males are lawyers. Their numbers in relation to the population as a whole have been rising for a decade, and now are rising more quickly than ever before.

In *The Human Condition* Hannah Arendt observed that there is a pendulum swing in human affairs between the individual and the institution. For a while, one is the focus for great concentrations of human energy and attention, then gradually the other focus takes over. We have been deep in the swing into and reliance on large institutional structures to shape and contain human affairs. The swing is now headed back the other way.

V: The Painful Present

What we are living through today may be a modern variant of what Asians call the "withdrawal of the mandate of heaven." This situation arose whenever an administration or regime lost the ability or desire to share with its people a sense of what was needed and what was just, and the capability to rule in accordance with those sensings. No one in particular ever said that the mandate was revoked; this feeling just gradually filtered through the people until it colored the overall climate of opinion. If in this condition a usurper from within or an invader from without threatened the regime, it would either crumble or be taken over intact like a hermit crab claiming a sea shell.

Today the mandate of heaven has been withdrawn

from the large institutions still configured in accordance with the 10 percent/90 percent human resource pyramid. As the 10 percent swells to 20 percent, 30 percent, 40 percent, more people feel that their own capabilities and the exercise of their own imaging functions are ignored or impeded by the institutional structures of the society rather than actively assisted and extended by them. While people's capacities are increasing, the opportunities to exercise them are not. There is a present need for institutions to reshape themselves or be supplanted by others in response to another immense increase in the "working capital" of the human race.

For a quick sense of what has happened, look at education (and particularly higher education) and where it has been left after the First Revolution. In the course of this revolution, learning functions were taken out of the family and workplace, where they were related to people living and producing and actually meeting their own and others' needs and wants, and moved into a separate educational setting, where learning became an end in itself (rather than the desirable by-product of other activities) and where it was assumed that learning took place primarily as a result of teaching. This tendency was not merely toward standardization but toward abstraction, toward generalizations valid in greater numbers of circumstances and away from the particular and concrete. Schools, in a word, taught theory whenever they could.

Schumacher once remarked that Mao Tse-tung's great contribution to the future might have been his insistence that good theory comes only from reflecting on real experience and not from others' theories. Yet here we constructed a huge educational edifice designed primarily around teaching theory rather than providing learning experiences, an edifice in fact dominated in terms of status by those who have been able to concentrate totally on theory and get away even from teaching.

An example of the dynamic that operated in the First Revolution: Here was something the 10 percent could do that was deeply gratifying, challenging, and fulfilling for them, and that also seemed to help the remaining 90 percent and to advance the society as a whole. But as the capacities and self-confidence of the acted-upon 90 percent expanded, they increasingly regarded as a kind of intellectual colonialism the fond attentions of the 10 percent. Theory, of course, is precisely the end product of imaging and experience—of acting, observing, reflecting, forming working hypotheses, acting to test them, revising them—that Brahma people want to work out for themselves. Thus the turmoil in educational institutions of the last twenty years: they have lost the mandate of heaven and have yet to find their new role.

Because we don't readily see that the pressures on the formerly effective and stable social institutions arise from our changing human resource pyramid, we have been slow to understand the true nature of the phenomenon taking place around us. In the new configuration, to make a case in point, the old political polarities no longer apply. The conservative and liberal mentalities as we usually think of them are opposite sides of the same coin. Both share an overreliance on the large centralized organization as the primary modality of effective human activity, though conservatives happen to put their faith in business corporations and liberals in government. Together they constitute the New Tories.

Working the other side of the street from what Schumacher called the "people of the onward stampede" are what he called "homecomers," people who more than anything else share a concern about the scale in their lives. They want to bring the perimeters in. Operate closer to home. They want to take responsibility for their lives and the effects of their activities both direct and indirect, and hence they tend to direct energy and attention—once they have had the experience of the macrosystems—toward things they can affect directly. This is still far from a conventional political force; many homecomers have digested the experience of what they regard as too many generations too sanguine about the ultimate effectiveness of primary reliance on power and on politics. They are only now beginning to find the commonalities among their disparate value systems and the connections they can make. What is happening is an immense diversity of individual and small-group imaging: the characteristic of Brahmas.

A neat example of "getting only what you asked for" occurred several years ago when the World Bank and the government of India collaborated on a series of huge projects designed to increase industrial production. What Thorstein Veblen called "trained incapacity" caused the experts involved to base all their assumptions on statistics derived from information collected only on factories or workshops employing ten or more people. Some time later it was discovered that almost half of the total industrial production of the country occurs in production units with fewer than ten workplaces. Much the same thing is going on here: The information nets of the dinosaurs are missing homecomer activities. In a few years our Internal Revenue Service will be tearing out its hair over the rising percentage of real productivity that through cash and barter and self-help and mutual aid transactions isn't showing up at all in the tax-collecting mechanisms.

Understanding the homecomers makes the passage of California's now-legendary Proposition 13 less puzzling. The sheer anomalousness of the "Prop 13" vote left politicians, intellectuals, and other social observers scrambling for explanations. The coalition against passage of Prop 13 was made up of over 130 of the most powerful organizations in the state, running a bewildering gamut from big corporations and organized labor, through professional organizations, all the way to minority and poverty organizations, Common Cause, environmentalists, and the rest of the liberal left. The only significant statewide organization in favor of Prop 13 was one farmers' organization. It seemed impossible that Prop 13 could win with so much "responsible" and "leadership" firepower against it. Yet it won in a landslide.

No one seemed to know what this meant, however. Because original sponsorship of Prop 13 came from deeply conservative political country in southern California, there has since been much useless talk about a "conservative resurgence" and the "politics of selfishness." But none of this hits the mark, and it surely doesn't help to explain the unusual facts involved. For instance, tens of thousands of government employees who rent homes rather than own them seemed to "vote twice" *contrary to their own apparent self-interest* by supporting Prop 13. Not only would they not benefit from the Prop 13 tax reductions, which were reserved for property owners, but their own jobs would doubtless be jeopardized if major reductions were forced in governmental spending and employment.

Voters in favor of Prop 13 might answer something like this if someone asked the right questions about their real motives:

"I resent your automatic assumption that I am turning my back on the poor, the elderly, the nonwhite, and others with impaired capacities or opportunities. I support many of the social and governmental mechanisms that have been evolved over the past two generations to redistribute income and meet human needs. But too many vast government programs do *to* people rather than *for* people, or do things for us in ways we don't want them done. They don't honor people's yearnings to do things for themselves; in fact, they deaden them. I would be willing to pay high taxes—even as high as the taxes in several European countries—if the money were used to support small-scale locally conceived and directed activities. I *am* sick and tired of having my taxes support a bloated, lazy, and smug bureaucracy and their

189

attendant legions of consultants and other professionals. I hear you say that Prop 13 is an indiscriminate 'meat-axe' approach to a situation too complex for me to understand. Well, friend, I think you professionals and civil servants have a vested interest in keeping the situation so complex that only you and your ilk can understand—or claim to understand—and deal with it. Maybe this is a brutal meat-axe approach. But I remember the man from Missouri who said that sometimes the only way to get a mule's attention is to pick up a two-by-four and hit him between the eyes."

Another place to find an indication of the forces operating within the bulging human resource pyramid is to look at the way people regard and respond to their work. For some time now there has been the assumption that (creative artists and farmers apart) all significant, rewarding, worthwhile, fulfilling work takes place within large organizations. This dependence of work on large systems applied even to many professionals who might on the surface appear to be "sole practitioners"; the medical doctor with hospital privileges and perhaps an adjunct teaching post at a medical school finds these organizations crucial to his standing as a leading member of his profession.

But there is daily evidence that fewer people are able to find rewarding work inside the organizational systems—work that engrosses their energies and engages their allegiance. It is not a matter of work roles getting "worse"; much brutalizing labor has been eliminated, and a white-collarization of the world is well under way. But satisfaction is lacking because a "sense of consequence" is lacking in specialized and fragmented activity in which we deal with only one piece of a process which leads either to a remote or even really undesirable achievement; and because the sense of responsibility is not engaged within productive activity. It has become a process outside and apart from our deepest motivations which satisfies none of the aspirations that to Brahma people become an increasingly urgent concern. In those circumstances, "dropouts in place" remain on the payroll but commit little or none of their vital energies and concerns to the enterprise. And of course in those circumstances the only thing left that can be satisfied is the pocketbook.

Schumacher believed that the growing distance between people and their work was a principal engine of inflation. As work becomes intrinsically less engaging and rewarding and challenging in terms of any sense of productivity of things really valued by people, our attention invariably shifts to getting more money for it. Thus the only way to solve inflation is to redesign work, the product and the process of production and often the structure of ownership or management of workplaces as well, so that work better reaches and provides productive expression for the deep motivations and wellsprings of human beings.

VI: The Meta-economy

One way to get a fix on the Hereford-into-Brahma movement is to look at work. As I said before, Brahmas

attach special importance to work and how their productive energies are engaged with the world. Because
economics revolves around the matter of work, it gives
us a language to begin expressing something of what is
taking place.

Right now I see in the United States the rise of a
meta-economy based on different principles, assumptions, and values than the ordinary economy. Think of
the meta-economy as reflecting the relative strengths of
two separate and competing economies: the "exhausting" economy of conventional economic theory, one
that exhausts not only people and resources but itself as
well (its rate of generation of real new jobs in relation to
population has been declining since the 1950s, of new
capital since the 1960s); and a "renewing" economy that
is trying to add a number of values to the economic
equation. Meta-economics concerns itself with the degree to which an economic transaction reflects the
deepest yearnings and motivations of the people who
are party to it.

The exhausting economy and conventional economics fail to distinguish between renewable and nonrenewable resources, thus confusing capital and income resources. The exhausting economy treats individuals as
labor or consumers, seldom as producers; it defines
people's productivity by the degree to which they serve
the interests of the organizations for which they work; it
measures the size, scope, and health of the economy by
numbers; and it fails to count many of the real human,
environmental, or social costs of particular technologies

or economic processes by dismissing them as "externalities."

The renewing economy, by contrast, starts from the crucial principle articulated by Schumacher and many others of the *oikonomos*, literally the household—not only the individual household where people serve one another's needs and wants, but the larger household of the earth itself, where all the necessary interdependencies must be recognized and observed. This is not a static economy. As Schumacher would say, it is stupid to talk about growth or nongrowth; we must talk about what kind of growth. The renewing economy sees a near limitless growth potential based on keeping the self-generating, self-regulating, self-disciplining productive capacities of human beings in full partnership with nature, where both are able to operate in accordance with the deepest laws governing their living and flowering.

To conventional economists, discussing an economy in these terms sounds like a lot of mystical hocus-pocus. But the hard evidence is beginning to show up in things like the number of people reorganizing their work lives, at substantial financial cost, to achieve a greater sense of consequence and sense of satisfaction about what they do.

Part of the comparison problem is that the two economies use different yardsticks to judge things: one measures money, the other measures value. For the conventional, the exhausting economy, the gross national product is the standard indicator. But the meta-economist will ask why the GNP includes the money a man spends when he goes out and buys a table for his family to eat dinner on, but ignores the productivity and generation of real "wealth" involved if he makes the table himself. Given that skew in the GNP, it is impossible, for example, to know the economic productivity that goes into making clothes at home. The best one can do is to extrapolate from the dimensions (very substantial, by the way) of the surely supportive activity that may show up in the GNP: sales of fabrics, findings, sewing machines, and patterns; enrollment in classes; and so forth.

In other words, much of what the meta-economist values does not show up in the conventional indicators. As Ralph Nader said, you contribute to the GNP when you run your car into someone else's; your contribution is still greater if you hurt the people inside. The renewing economy, by contrast, attempts to maximize the net positive *real* effects of economic transactions, particularly as measured by their impact on the positive partnership of mankind and nature. Monetized transactions are not regarded as the significant measure of economic activity; at most they are the shadows thrown by a much larger reality with a different shape.

Today these two overlapping economies are competing with one another for people's allegiance. Each individual or family decision about the use of its imagination and energy and resources will strengthen one economy and weaken the other. The two economies compete, essentially, to prove which over time can help the largest number of people to make their livelihood in ways they find rewarding.

It is valid to think of the exhausting economy as the setting in which Hereford people hold jobs to make a living, and the renewing economy as the setting and state of mind in which Brahma people create workplaces while pursuing their livelihood.

Work in the exhausting economy is a monetized transaction. A person is paid wages, salary, or a fee for his services; this money is paid out in turn to others who supply one's needs or wants because one's own work doesn't directly contribute anything to meeting them. In recent years, people have been seeking a more tangible sense of productivity in their lives. In great numbers they have been moving back to the land or otherwise back toward primary and secondary production. In doing so, though most of them are still in a transitional stage, they are leaving the exhausting economy and joining the renewing economy.

A crude reflection of this process is contained in census figures. The ten states that lost the most population in the 1960 census, most of them rural, were in 1970 at or near the top of the list of those gaining population. At first this was thought to be a Sun Belt phenomenon of more people retiring early and seeking their ease in pleasant surroundings. But now it seems that these are people making *working* lives in rural areas and smaller communities, including the rainy Northwest and cold Northeast.

By the hundreds of thousands, people are trying to

reorder their lives in a new economic balance that often contains four elements:

(a) Producing goods (crops, furniture, house, clothing, etc.) to meet the needs and wants of one's own family;

(b) Producing goods or services that one sells (or barters) directly to other people for whatever currency is agreed on, rather than selling one's services to an institution;

(c) Investing money, thought, and effort in resources that reduce one's present or future need for money payout and consequent dependence on macrosystems (e.g., installing solar panels, wood stoves, windmills, etc.);

(d) Reducing to lifeline status one's connection to and participation in the professional or technical or administrative work that is executed for money (usually in an urban setting, usually for a large organization, usually in a knowledge-related form of activity).

This trend catches the social theorists by surprise. It flies in the face of the predictions made by Daniel Bell, Herman Kahn, and other theorists of the post-industrial society. They felt they had found an essential dynamic: the steady movement of people out of the primary and secondary sectors of human activity and into tertiary, quaternary, and even quinquenary sectors.* Of course

*Primary production is directly in contact with nature: farming, fishing, timbering, mining. Secondary production is generally manufacturing. Until recently, tertiary activity covered everything else: sales, distribution, marketing, services of all kinds. Now the tertiary is being carved up into subsections: if the tertiary sector is services, then the quaternary is services-to-services and the quinquenary might be services-to-services-to-services (such as the people who organize conferences for those who provide training services for salespeople).

this looked like a good thing. These men were writing in the fullest flush of excitement over assemblage of an entire knowledge industry composed of education, communications, the professions, publishing and the media, and other information- and idea-related services. It seemed that the pull of these "clean" jobs would be irresistible to people and that the economy would continue to flow in that direction.

What the post-industrial theorists overlooked was this: A population with a far greater degree of Brahma blood will find white-collar organizational jobs as limiting and stultifying as an earlier generation found factory work. People have been pulling back from abstract knowledge work for some time, though now the flow is strong enough to register on some of the social seismographs. Their knowledge-related work, these people say, lacks a sense of consequence; they have lost the feeling that their fragmented or specialized or abstract contribution leads sufficiently directly to a result that is real, that has positive value in meeting the needs and wants of people, and that is relatively free of hidden or later-manifesting negative consequences.

In order to see where these new trends may be leading us, it is useful to give the meta-economy a graphic expression. The accompanying figure helps to suggest the pattern of operation of the whole meta-economy or of any mini-economy (such as the production or use of one thing) within it.

Begin with the idea of three sectors or "markets" in the economy:

Sector "A" is the subsistence or expenditure-reducing

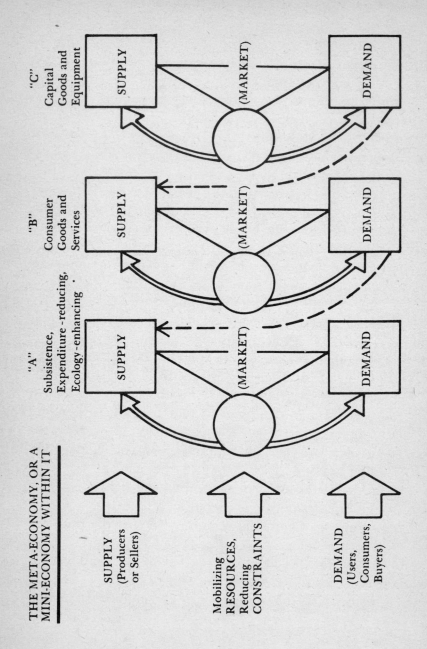

THE META-ECONOMY, OR A
MINI-ECONOMY WITHIN IT

SUPPLY
(Producers
or Sellers)

Mobilizing
RESOURCES,
Reducing
CONSTRAINTS

DEMAND
(Users,
Consumers,
Buyers)

"A"
Subsistence,
Expenditure - reducing,
Ecology - enhancing

SUPPLY

(MARKET)

DEMAND

"B"
Consumer
Goods and
Services

SUPPLY

(MARKET)

DEMAND

"C"
Capital
Goods and
Equipment

SUPPLY

(MARKET)

DEMAND

sector. People here do not earn monetary income but they do create real wealth in conventional economic terms to meet their own needs (growing their food, making their clothes) or to exchange with others (growing extra food). They also reduce their need for monetary outgo through reliance on wood stoves, windmills, and so forth. (I also include here what I think of as ecology-enhancing activities, those which produce "psychic income" by making one feel less of a burden or disruption to nature: e.g., buying and maintaining older vehicles rather than new ones with their massive energy cost, even though that action is "uneconomic" by traditional calculations.)

Sector "B" is the monetized consumer goods and services market, where people gain monetary income by producing goods or services for sale to others.

Sector "C" is the capital goods and equipment sector, where people produce the technologies (broadly defined) or raw materials or other factor inputs needed by those who would become producers in the "B" sector (or sometimes even in the "A" sector).

The dotted lines represent the movement of people and technologies into different roles in the three sectors. Someone who buys a shovel acts as the demand end of sector "B." But then he takes the shovel over to sector "A" and becomes a producer with it at the supply end, by using it to help grow food. Or one buys a wool-spinning machine at the demand end of sector "C" and produces yarn with it (supply end of sector "B") for sale (demand end of "B"). (As one starts to play with specific actions and technologies, it becomes evident there ought

199

to be more dotted lines—for instance, that spinning machine might also produce the yarn you use to make your own clothes, in sector "A." But the diagram is complicated enough already.)

Each sector is a market where one person's production is supply to meet another person's needs or wants (in sector "A," of course, one is meeting one's own needs, so supply and demand are one party). But each market has a third aspect that regulates supply and demand and the growth of the market as a whole. This third corner in the market relates to the mobilization of resources (getting access to land or capital, or getting a badly needed new lower-capital-cost technology designed and produced) and the reduction of constraints (getting a zoning variance so that a small farm can contain both agriculture and a small industry).

In any given market, supply cannot develop much beyond the current demand or the supplier will go bankrupt; similarly, demand cannot develop much ahead of the current supply, because what the buyer would need simply would not be there yet. Growth depends on a positive climate that encourages a constant back-and-forth readjustment of supply and demand to one another. But because the third corner—the constraints and the control of resources—still reflects mainly the needs of the exhausting economy and its institutions, many of the mini-economies in the meta-economy are still fragile and have yet to make their presence really felt.

This can be seen more clearly in an example like the market in composting toilets. The producer of composting toilets is in the supply side of sector "B." The buyer is on the demand side of "B" until he puts the toilet to use, presumably in the "A" sector (unless of course he sells the compost, in which case he would be using this technology to be a producer in sector "B").

Composting toilets reflect the "chicken and egg" relationship of supply and demand. Producers won't sell many toilets until more people know about them; and buyers won't find a diverse and quality-competitive selection (which in turn will increase motivation to buy) until the market is mature enough to provide technically practical and economically viable models at a reasonable cost per unit. But this mini-economy shows exceptionally well the influence of the resources-and-constraints corner of the market. The composting toilet mini-economy will remain severely limited until three things begin to happen in a fair number of communities: building and health codes change to permit (or encourage) the installation and use of composting toilets; banks and other financial institutions make new construction and remodeling loans to finance their installation; federal and local governments give tax benefits to those who install composting toilets *and* impose tax penalties on those who do not.

One last point about the three sectors: In general, the "B" sector requires higher front-end and operating investments (money, equipment, specialized knowledge, management skills, minimum number of workplaces) than the "A" sector. The "C" sector, with rare exceptions (for instance, the capital equipment in some mature handcraft industries such as looms), requires yet higher investments in larger or more complex ventures with consequent greater risk-taking than enterprises in the "B" sector.

This picture gives me a way to understand what is happening in the overall meta-economy and in the particular precincts concerned with self-sufficiency, decentralization, and appropriate technology. About 85 percent of the activity, in terms of its economic significance or effect, lies in the "A" sector; 10 to 15 percent in the "B" sector; and 1 percent—if that—in the "C" sector. By and large the "C" sector has been left to the tender mercies and initiatives (or lack of them) of the industrial sector of the existing exhausting economy.

The result is a condition that Schumacher called the Law of the Disappearing Middle. The primitive or traditional or very low cost technologies always remain (a hoe is not likely to become obsolete) but are of low productivity. At the other end of the spectrum, the state-of-the-art technologies grow ever larger, more complex, more capital costly. And they tend to drive out of existence, out of production, and out of the market where people could buy them and use them to make their livelihood the smaller and cheaper technologies in the middle.

For the meta-economy to mature, it will need to develop or rediscover lower capital cost, intermediate scale production technologies that allow people to engage in direct production activities, thereby reducing or eliminating their dependence on the macroeconomy.

If the meta-economy is to move beyond its educated-middle-class beginnings, it will have to demonstrate its capacity to bring more people within its borders to make their livelihoods. Practically, this means developing the "C" sector in accordance with the principles of the meta-economy, as well as the "A" and "B" sectors.

If this happens, if the meta-economy begins to produce and market its own technologies that allow people to function productively outside the customary wage structure and thereby to diversify and strengthen their own family microeconomies, then the eventual results could be truly earthshaking. Schumacher often said that Gandhi would be rated by history as not only a great religious and political leader but a great development economist. He would then cite Gandhi's statement that what the world needed, not merely India but all nations including the industrialized ones, was "not mass production but production by the masses."

For the first time in history, this may be about to happen as it becomes feasible in technological and economic terms—which means, crucial to everything, in human terms. Where the change in the nature of human beings and their awareness of the expansion of their own capacities—the Hereford-into-Brahma shift—is combined with the development of benign technologies and diversified opportunities to exercise this enormous increase in human productive capacities—the development of the meta-economy— then true *production by the masses* undertaken largely under their own initiative and their own control is not only possible and feasible but imperative.

VII: How to Find Good Work

Where has all this brought us?

We have seen that far greater numbers of human beings are developing a greatly expanded sense of their own capacities and that this places a strain on the social apparatus because these people also have greater requirements: they want to get more out of life by putting more into life.

We have seen that the institutions and organizations geared to an earlier state of the human resource pyramid cannot adequately absorb or respond to this flowering of capacity. The result is a growing number of people who are not engaged, engrossed, or challenged by their large-organizational roles and who are yearning for some form of good work.

Finally we have seen the beginnings of a new economy that will be capable of supporting good work, of giving productive form not just to people's extended capacities but to their desire to engage these capacities in the world in a rewarding and positive fashion.

There is in the world today, then, both the necessity and the opportunity for more and more people to find good work.

But the finding may not be easy in the individual case. A person experiencing these forces in his or her own life will feel buffeted, insecure, isolated. Even in the quickest and easiest circumstance, a realignment of one's life involves a period of withdrawal from the accepted realities, followed by a period of rethinking goals, and only then a wholehearted new engagement with things.

THE MAKING OF GOOD WORK

In each phase the frustration and swirl of negative energies may obscure the positive things happening underneath. It is a difficult time and kind of transition, not only socially but individually.

I have been through some of these changes in my own life. My work with Schumacher has brought me in contact with many hundreds of otherwise ordinary people who are living through their versions of these changes. Many of them are extraordinary and courageous in their lives and work in a way that quickens my heart and thickens my throat. So from that perspective, let me say a few things about how to order, understand, and express creatively these forces when they blow in through some newly opened door in your life.

In the question periods after his talks, Schumacher would invariably get asked by someone in the audience, "But what can *I* do?" His simple answer was "Do three things, one after the other, one leading into the other. Inform yourself. Support others who are already at work. Initiate where you can and how you can." And he said something else: "Start where you are. But *start*. Don't wait for the perfect situation."

Inform yourself. Accept the necessity that you will have to begin consciously building your own new map of reality. There are some good books and commanding minds to help you in that process. Leopold Kohr *(The Overdeveloped Nations: The Diseconomies of Scale)* was the man who helped Schumacher clarify his understanding of scale and the tendency of ever-larger systems to create ever-larger problems. Wendell Berry *(The Unsettling of America)* combines a soaring ecological and philosophical vision with detailed knowledge of how industrialized agriculture is failing us. Hazel Henderson *(Creating Alternative Futures: The End of Economics)* is an original and blindingly powerful economist and social thinker whose analytical and prescriptive vision dovetails with Schumacher's. Amory Lovins *(Soft Energy Paths)* is a physicist who has carried energy analysis into new political and social realms. Edgar L. Owens *(Development Reconsidered)* wrote a book about the third world that includes much of depth and importance for us to understand about industrialized countries too. John Todd of the New Alchemy Institute is a marine biologist and appropriate technologist with far-reaching vision. Scott Burns *(Home, Inc.,* and *The Household Economy)* is an imaginative wizard with statistics who is able to make tangible the real and growing power of the meta-economy. These people and books will lead you to another dozen first-class minds working along similar lines.

There are also marvelous periodicals, and here I am familiar with only the tip of the iceberg. Every one of these is worth not merely the price of a subscription but of buying if you can five years' back issues (when you consider their combined circulation figures you get a rough idea of the dimensions of the meta-economy and how fast human attention, aspiration, and energy are moving in this direction).

In a philosophical and metaphysical sense, *MANAS* is the benign grandfather brooding over much of this universe, the journal that published Richard Gregg's pivotal "Voluntary Simplicity" article thirty years ago and began publishing Schumacher in the early 1960s, almost ten years before any other American publication. Schumacher considered the British *Studies in Comparative Religion* the other most important periodical he read.

There is Stewart Brand's *CoEvolution Quarterly*, successor to his *Whole Earth Catalog*, where the "back of the book" constantly updates the *Catalog* and the front reaches out to new frontiers. John Shuttleworth's *Mother Earth News, Blair and Ketchum's Country Journal,* John Cole's *Maine Times*, Charles Walters's *Acres U.S.A.*, and Bob Rodale's two titans, *Prevention* and *Organic Gardening and Farming,* all are packed with information about what real people are already doing in, or headed toward, the meta-economy. From time to time each also contains absolutely first-class thinking.

There are scores of lesser-known individuals and small groups doing real work of almost unimaginable importance. I think of the small scale farming work of John Jeavons in Palo Alto, California, who is achieving incredible yields per square foot (or, equally significant in the world we face, per gallon of water) using biodynamic–French intensive techniques of Alan Chadwick's, partly derived from Rudolf Steiner's work. Almost more important, Jeavons's meticulous recording of work, water, and other inputs and weighing of yields is helping to lay the base of a key discipline in the meta-economy, the agricultural economics of more biological as contrasted with heavily chemical agriculture.

Support others. Buy or borrow a suitcaseful of these

publications, get an atlas and some colored felt pens, and spend weekday evenings for three months marking up the atlas to connect real people with real places. The world will look entirely different to you. Whenever you learn about some interesting project, think of it as part of a specific mini-economy in terms of what is produced and used, where and how it is produced, and what part it plays in which sector both of the mini-economy and of the specific local economy. Think too of the other corners and other "markets" in that mini-economy, who it could buy from or sell to whom (or barter), where needs and opportunities may coincide where you might go to work.

Use your purchasing power selectively, both to inform yourself and to support good work in being. Think about how a given purchase or transaction serves to strengthen the meta-economy or the exhausting economy, how it can be targeted to strengthen something or someone you want to support. Remember Gandhi's remark that if your village barber gives a bad haircut, instead of going to Madras for a haircut from a city barber it is better to patronize the village barber and persuade him to learn how to give a better haircut. All of these things take effort as they become conscious, deliberate economic acts; they also take on reality in your own mind and give meaning where none existed.

Pay dues to the half-dozen groups closest to your place (where you are or where you might want to move to) or to your specific interests as you start to identify them through daydreaming. Get yourself invited to one of their work weekends. Do anything that needs doing on the first day; it may be rough or boring, but you thereby pay your dues so you can spend some time the next day poking around and asking questions. Find out what things they wish they could do next "if only." Think constantly in terms of mini-economies, local economies, and diversifying personal and family microeconomies (your own and others'). Identify where you might provide or help find the "if only" for them. Add more pages to your notebook, and mark up your atlas some more as your own map of reality, conceptual and factual, starts to feed on itself and to grow and reach out.

Remember the three different groups of home-comers—those who remain within the macro-institutions, those who work on them from the out-side, and those who go off into the meta-economy—and realize how much they need to work with each other (the second category often provides valuable skills for reducing constraints in any sector or "market" of a mini-economy: getting county commissioners to give a variance or change a regulation, for instance). You will need to understand the strengths and capabilities and mind-set of each to help bring them together where you can.

Don't be put off by the number of people whose professional expertise causes them to focus on a *problem* rather than on the potential resources to solve it or prevent it from arising in the first place; that is one of the problems with professionalization. And don't be put off by the extraordinary number of people with good motivation and underused vital energies whose initial idea of the way to make a constructive contribution is criticism.

Keep in mind the lethal summary of our whole situation that Hazel Henderson encountered in a bona fide serious question after one of her talks: "Where do you get federal funding for projects in self-reliance?" Our unconscious dependence on or at least deference to large organizations, the legacy of the assumption that nothing effective happens except through their participation, is in our bloodstream. Self-immunization takes prolonged and constant attention to unexamined assumptions, questioning, clearing away, letting the new and stronger emerge.

Combine your informing and supporting activities with others as you find them, pooling information and resources, ideas and energies and questions. You can contribute up to 10 percent of your income to existing nonprofit organizations (or new ones you form). You can invest more money and have it deductible by "losing" it in some kind of business enterprise that is pointed toward becoming a viable part of some corner of some sector of some mini-economy—so long as the endeavor makes basic economic sense and is making progress toward break-even. Good, imaginative, and principled lawyers and accountants love to help on projects like this, where the government subsidizes your work whether they like it or not.

Initiate your own things. Here I would add another component to Schumacher's urgent dictum "Take back the value added," namely "Take back the imaging function." By imaging I mean that aspect of imagination which seeks a resulting action in the real world. As much as humanly possible, the crucial imaging function must be conducted by those who will actually make the entrepreneurial leap from thought to action, venturing their energies and resources and often their working lives. Professionals and specialists typically think that it is a regrettable waste of everyone's time when people "have to reinvent the wheel." The essential fact to the contrary is that professionals, specialists, and experts (few of whom, we might note, also have responsibility for any real action or risk-taking) have eliminated the imaging function, *when going through that imaging process is an essential precondition for the mobilization of thought and action and self-discipline required to carry through anything of any substance and complexity,* most particularly any real business or any other productive economic process.

In the case of the urban professional or other knowledge person who is trying to find or create his or her own good work—or at least the part of it that comes from diversifying one's personal or family micro-economy—in a rural area or smaller community, then that is where the imaging must be done. Going beyond the assemblage of experience and information to the formulation of actual what-if working hypotheses, which are then tested until one of them gains enough weight and validity to be put into action—this all requires a focus on place, people, and local economy and mini-economy in the actual environment where the work will take place.

One of the best ways to stoke the imaging fires is by

means of County Self-Studies. The idea is to look at the county as if it were an independent island republic. What do we produce here? What do we consume or use? Where does it come from? What could we produce that we don't produce now? How could we meet more of our own needs? How can we diversify the local economy?

The County Self-Studies are usually conducted by self-selected pick-up groups of local people who together want to generate a picture of their local reality and potentials based on meta-economic principles and geared to locating new enterprises. The area doesn't specifically need to be a county. There should be a large enough mass of land and people to provide a diversity of mutually reinforcing conjectures, yet it should be small enough so that people can meet together frequently and bear the expense out of their own pockets. Sometimes a useful study can be made on the basis of a Congressional district. There is an enormous amount of information available from the federal government already "broken out" on a district basis; because of reapportionment each district has about half a million people and therefore what has been done in one district may have direct usefulness to people in another. Most important, perhaps, the project has a built-in interested audience of one, its member of Congress, for whom almost nothing generated from his or her own constituents is ever hand-tailored to his capacities to act.

The past of the locality and its economy can provide enormous resources of experience and information and ideas. These are "tailings" that can be "mined" by the present generation for concrete and relevant possibilities for economic activities that, for instance, once went on in this area but went out of business in the 1930s because of competition from the outside, which is now losing its competitive advantage as transport costs rise.

There are four streams of existing activity and vitality (though we may need to be encouraged or assisted to shift our attention toward identifying additional ways in which people might make their livelihood in the local economy):

(a) The local history projects that gained vitality around the United States at the time of the 1976 Bicentennial;

(b) The oral history and other projects along the line of the "Foxfire" program in Georgia, seeking—often with teenagers interviewing their elders—to preserve and recapture local folk skills and rural technologies;

(c) The "industrial archaeology" projects that have proliferated all over the British Isles and Western Europe and have a number of counterparts in the United States and Canada, in which older mills and industrial plants and other technologies are excavated, repaired, and brought back into production either intermittently as tourist/educational resources or on a continuous and economically viable basis; and

(d) The vast resources of knowledge and ideas represented by the professional historians of technology to be found in universities and museums in almost every corner of North America.

These County Self-Studies are not antiquarian exercises. They aim at stockpiling past experience and present knowledge and imagination and conjecture in

order to provide raw materials for the imaging processes of those people who must actually make individual decisions to take one particular possibility and
run with it. They must be kept open and comprehensi-
ble to the ordinary public. They cannot be institu-
tionalized or put into the hands of paid professionals;
even academics and professionals and other sources of
knowledge who yearn to help must learn to be "on tap,
not on top." Existing prototypes suggest that teenagers
and retired people between them often provide the best
staffing and direction for such studies at minimal financial cost and with minimal institutional structure.

Once the imaging of the potential "entrepreneurs"—based in part on the raw materials stock-
piled by the self-studies—has led to concrete decisions
and commitments, another type of locally generated
and directed institution can come into play. George
McRobie, Schumacher's closest longtime associate in
Britain, has been taking the leadership there with John
Davis in helping stimulate and encourage the formation
of what they call Local Enterprise Trusts. Here, by
contrast with the self-studies, there is a slightly higher
level of professionalization, though still the maximum
resistance both to salaried staffs and elaborate institutional structures. People working through Local Enterprise Trusts generally have some concrete experience in
small or large business, government, or a relevant
profession such as law or accounting. Their role is to
bring to bear capital and professional, technical and
specialized help when the actual venturers need it and
ask for it.

Such a Local Enterprise Trust is often nonprofit but concerned with helping both conventional for-profit businesses and other patterns of enterprise (such as production cooperatives or worker-owned or community-owned corporations) to succeed and flourish. It is frequently able to invest locally generated capital in such an enterprise, lend assistance sufficient to help make the enterprise a success, and then conclude its "grassroots investment banking" role by letting itself be bought out at an early stage and returning the capital thus recouped to a revolving fund for the assistance of newer enterprises.

The dynamic underlying the whole thing is the process of people taking back the imaging function.

Frequently people at his lectures seemed disappointed with Schumacher's answer to their "What can I do?" They appeared to want something quicker and easier and more painless than the inform-support-initiate process. What I fear they have not yet realized is the degree to which good work is an inner program. There is no outer prescription, course, or exercise that will bring a person to good work. We find it from the inside out.

Work is good when it engages what Huston Smith and others have called "the vertical dimension" of life, the deepest and highest values and motivations that underlie the universe and all human life and activity. To see work as a day-to-day expression of value makes it of far more than economic significance. Then it is no less than the place where our temporal and spiritual dimensions converge to create acts in the world. When those possibilities are blocked or lost, the personal costs are invariably great.

Schumacher may have been trying to catch some of this in a phrase that he used two or three times in the last year of his life. The words resonate in the back of my mind, and in my spirit, almost to the point where they could be said to haunt me. If you know something, he said, really *know* it, and don't *act* on it, then it will go sour on you, it will fester inside you.

VIII: On Understanding History

The need to understand the cycles of history is no mere intellectual hobby for me. I am a white Anglo-Saxon Protestant with an unruly dash of Celtic on the side. I am also male, educated, and professionally experienced, and now middle-aged. To make my own peace with the recent past, I need to know why the traditions I find represented in my own life suddenly seem so inadequate if not destructive. It is a matter of coming to terms with my antecedents.

In the long slow process of consideration and speculation, I have been struck by the following characteristics of the modern world:

- The discovery and use of great, often explosive, new powers that did not exist or were not realized before;
- A fascination and excitement with using these powers and a tendency to believe—contrary to the

216

traditional wisdom of mankind—that if something is exciting, it is therefore valid and valuable;

- A strong disposition, in exploring and using these extended powers, not to think about—even resolutely to ignore—the consequences of employing such forces or manipulative capacities;

- A sense that there is nothing to learn from the past—indeed, a belief that the value systems from which we come are holding us back, constricting or stultifying us; and

- A tendency to be quite vocal about the positive values we espouse and to think ourselves unique in this regard, often to a degree that other, older traditions find abrasive.

Put in a personal frame of reference, these characteristics may begin to sound familiar to any adult: first the need to transcend and even deny one's roots, then later a kind of willing rejoining of one's own stream of growth, now defined and strong, with the river of time.

Perhaps these turbulent and confusing generations are carrying us through the worst of the adolescence of mankind.

Those who wish to make contact with organizations seeking to embody in action the values and concepts expressed in *Good Work* may write to:

Intermediate Technology Development Group, Ltd.
9 King Street
Covent Garden
London WC2, England

The Soil Association
Walnut Tree Manor
Haughley
Stowmarket
Suffolk, England

Intermediate Technology
556 Santa Cruz Avenue
Menlo Park, California 92045

INDEX

INDEX

Frederick Douglas
"The Narrative of a
Slave"

"food hire yourself
an employer"
R. K. Irish